# A Nation of States

RAND M⌐NALLY PUBLIC AFFAIRS SERIES

# A Nation

Essays on the American

BY

MORTON GRODZINS AND DANIEL ELAZAR
MARTIN DIAMOND
RUSSELL KIRK
HERBERT J. STORING
JAMES JACKSON KILPATRICK
HARRY V. JAFFA
WALTER BERNS

# of States

Federal System

SECOND EDITION

EDITED BY
Robert A. Goldwin

RAND MCNALLY COLLEGE PUBLISHING COMPANY ● CHICAGO

*The essays in this volume were prepared
as part of the program of the Public
Affairs Conference Center at
Kenyon College, Gambier, Ohio*

RAND MᶜNALLY PUBLIC AFFAIRS SERIES
Robert A. Goldwin, Series Editor

Edited by Robert A. Goldwin
America Armed: Essays on United States Military Policy
A Nation of States: Essays on the American Federal System
Why Foreign Aid?
Political Parties, U.S.A.
Left, Right and Center: Essays on Liberalism and Conserv-
atism in the United States
Higher Education and Modern Democracy: The Crisis of
the Few and the Many
A Nation of Cities: Essays on America's Urban Problems
Representation and Misrepresentation: Legislative
Reapportionment in Theory and Practice
On Civil Disobedience: American Essays Old and New
How Democratic Is America? Responses to the New
Left Challenge

Edited by Harry M. Clor
Censorship and Freedom of Expression: Essays on Obscenity
and the Law
Civil Disorder and Violence: Essays on Causes and Cures
The Mass Media and Modern Democracy

# PREFACE

●

Perhaps no other aspect of American politics is so much discussed in theoretical and historical terms as is our federal system. The question of the legitimate powers of the respective governments— national, state, and local—arises in an amazing variety of political debates in the course of the day-to-day work of governing the United States. It appears in many guises, but federalism's presence is nonetheless unmistakable when we debate such diverse matters as civil rights, sharing of tax revenues, highway construction programs, labor laws, race relations, the farm problem, legislative redistricting, school construction, welfare programs—and so on in an interminable list.

The federalism issue is inescapable. It is built into our Constitution. Because of it, government officials must turn constantly to a reconsideration of the origins and foundations of our republic. As practical-minded as are the men who legislate and administer our laws at every level of government, they find themselves compelled, even when they have before them a project no more lofty than the disposal of sewage, to reflect on such matters as conflicting theories of federalism, opposing doctrines of constitutional interpretation, and even the remote and mysterious "intentions of the Founding Fathers."

Our federal system is thus a kind of school for statesmen; to do their work well they must seek out and study, again and again, the underlying principles of our form of government. But to state the necessity does not imply that the seeking is often fruitful or the study sound. After so many years and so many scholars and statesmen, the federal system remains very much a subject of puzzlement and uncertainty.

The authors of the present essays examine the American federal system in very different ways and their findings differ as much as their manners of approach. But the reader will find that the authors are in concurrence on two main points: first, that the successful governing of the American people requires an understanding of the federal structure of our political system; and, second, that there is today a profound misunderstanding and even gross ignorance of its essential character. In proportion as federalism has elicited an appeal to theory and history, so it has suffered distortion of principle and fact.

As with many great human institutions, our federal system can be defended and preserved only by those who understand it; knowledge is indispensable to its survival. In our time especially, to remain ignorant of the true nature of our government is to risk its destruction and thereby the loss of that liberty and justice of which it is both the temple and the fortress.

R. A. G.

November, 1962

# PREFACE TO THE SECOND EDITION

•

Several of the essays in this volume have been revised for the second edition. Some of the revisions are designed to take account of developments in American federalism during the past decade; others are designed to present additional perspectives. But the purpose and underlying themes of the volume remain the same. The reader is presented with a variety of systematically developed viewpoints which, taken together, constitute a debate about the basic principles and problems of the federal system in the United States.

**R. A. G.**

Brussels, Belgium
November, 1973

# CONTENTS

●

# CONTENTS

# THE EDITOR AND THE AUTHORS

ROBERT A. GOLDWIN

is Special Advisor to the United States Ambassador to NATO. He has been Dean of St. John's College, Annapolis, Maryland; Associate Professor of Political Science, Kenyon College; Director of the Public Affairs Conference Center, Kenyon College; and Editor of the Rand McNally Public Affairs Series. His fields of study include American political thought and political philosophy. His essay on "John Locke" appears in *History of Political Philosophy*, 1963. His edited books include *Political Parties, USA*, 1964; *Beyond the Cold War*, 1965; *Higher Education and Modern Democracy*, 1967 and *How Democratic Is America?*, 1971.

MORTON GRODZINS

Late Professor of Political Science and Director of the Federalism Workshop, The University of Chicago. His special field of study has been American political parties. His books include *Americans Betrayed*, 1949; *The Loyal and the Disloyal*, 1956; and (co-author) *Government and Housing in Metropolitan Areas*, 1958.

DANIEL J. ELAZAR

is Professor of Political Science and Director of the Center for the Study of Federalism, Temple University. His major fields of interest are American federalism and metropolitan politics. In 1960 he received the Leonard D. White Memorial Award of the American Political Science Association. His books include *The American Partnership*, 1962; *American Federalism: A*

*View from the States*, 1966; *Cities of the Prairie*, 1972; and *The Politics of Belleville*, 1971.

MARTIN DIAMOND
is Professor of Political Science, Northern Illinois University. He has been Burnet C. Wohlford Professor of American Political Institutions, Claremont Men's College and Claremont Graduate School, Claremont, California, and Chairman of the Political Science Department, Claremont Men's College. Professor Diamond is senior editor and co-author (with Winston M. Fisk and Herbert Garfinkel) of *The Democratic Republic: An Introduction to American Government*, 1966, and is the author of many articles and essays, including "Democracy and the Federalist: A Reconsideration of the Framers' Intent," *American Political Science Review*, 1959; chapter on The Federalist in *History of Political Philosophy*, 1963; and "Conservatives, Liberals, and the Constitution," in *Left, Right and Center*, 1967.

RUSSELL KIRK
is the author of *The Conservative Mind*, 1953; *Academic Freedom*, 1955; *Beyond the Dreams of Avarice*, 1956; *Edmund Burke*, 1967; *Enemies of the Permanent Things*, 1969; and many articles and essays. He has been Professor of Political Science at Long Island University and has taught at a number of universities and colleges.

HERBERT J. STORING
is Professor of Political Science, The University of Chicago. His special interests include public administration, the American presidency and Constitutional law. He is the author of essays on the thought of Booker T. Washington and Frederick Douglass. His books include *Essays on the Scientific Study of Politics* (editor and contributing author), 1962; and *The Anti-Federalist*, University of Chicago Press.

JAMES JACKSON KILPATRICK
is a journalist, national syndicated columnist and contributing editor of the *National Review*. He has been editor of the Rich-

mond (Virginia) *News Leader;* and is the author of *The Sovereign States: Notes of a Citizen of Virginia,* 1957; and *The Southern Case for School Segregation,* 1962.

HARRY V. JAFFA

is Professor of Political Philosophy, Claremont Men's College and Claremont Graduate School. His special interests are political philosophy and American politics. He is the author of *Thomism and Aristotelianism,* 1952; *Crisis of the House Divided,* 1959; *Equality and Liberty,* 1965; co-author (with Allan Bloom) of *Shakespeare's Politics,* 1964; contributing author of *History of Political Philosophy,* 1963; and co-editor (with Robert W. Johannsen) of *In the Name of the People,* 1959.

WALTER BERNS

is Professor of Political Science, University of Toronto. He has been Professor of Government, Cornell University, and Chairman of the Department of Government, Cornell University. He is the author of *Freedom, Virtue and the First Amendment,* 1957; *Constitutional Cases in American Government,* 1963; "Voting Studies," in *Essays in the Scientific Study of Politics,* 1962; and "Democracy, Censorship and the Arts," in *Censorship and Freedom of Expression,* 1971.

Morton Grodzins

Daniel Elazar

●

# CENTRALIZATION AND DECENTRALIZATION IN THE AMERICAN FEDERAL SYSTEM*

## I. The Marble Cake of American Government

To put the matter bluntly, government in the United States is chaotic. In addition to the central government and the fifty states, there are something like 18,000 general-purpose municipalities, almost an equal number of general-purpose townships, more than 3,000 counties, and so many special-purpose governments that no one can claim even to have counted them accurately. At an educated guess, there are some 81,000 tax-levying governments in the country. Single citizens may be buried under a whole pyramid of governments. A resident of Park Forest, Illinois, for example, though he may know very little else about them, knows that he pays taxes to eleven governments. The Park Forest citizen enjoys more governments than most people in the United States, but he is by no means unique. Though no one has made the exact calculation, it is not unlikely that a majority of citizens are within the jurisdiction of four or more governments, not counting the state and national ones.

The multitude of governments does not mask any simplicity of activity. There is no neat division of functions among them. If one looks closely, it appears that virtually all governments are involved in virtually all functions. More precisely, there is hardly any activity that does not involve the federal, state, and some local government

* This essay was originally prepared by Professor Morton Grodzins. It has been revised for the second edition of this volume by Daniel Elazar.

in important responsibilities. Functions of the American governments are shared. Consider a case that seems least likely to demonstrate the point: the function of providing education. It is widely believed that education is uniquely a local responsibility, the province of governments especially created for that purpose. A quarter of all governments in the United States are school districts. Is this a great simplifying fact? Does it indicate a focusing of educational responsibility in the hands of single-purpose local governments?

The answer to both questions is a clear "no." That there exist something like 21,000 school districts in the United States does not indicate that education, even in the elementary and high schools, is in any sense an exclusive function of those districts. In several states, local districts are administrative arms of state departments of education, and the educational function is principally a state responsibility. In all states, to a greater or lesser degree—and the degree tends to be greater—local districts are dependent upon state financial aid, state teacher certification, state prescription of textbooks, and state inspection of performance in areas as diverse as janitorial services and the caliber of Latin instruction. School districts also have intricate and diverse relationships with county and city governments. The latter, for example, often act as tax-levying and tax-collecting agencies for the districts; they are responsible for certifying that standards of health and safety are maintained on school property; they must provide special police protection to students.

Nor does the federal government play an unimportant role. Even prior to the Elementary and Secondary Education Act of 1964, the United States Office of Education provided technical aids of all sorts. Since the passing of that act, the federal role has become even more clear-cut. A federal milk and school-lunch program supplies food and milk at low cost to children in all fifty states. Federal surplus property supplies many essentials of school equipment. Federal aid to vocational and agricultural education programs make possible the employment of special teachers. In many areas "affected" by national government installations, federal funds build and maintain school buildings and contribute to general school support. Federal aid trains high-school teachers of science, mathematics, and foreign languages; contributes equipment and books for instruction in these fields; makes possible testing and guidance programs for the identification of superior students; provides special assistance for schools in poverty areas; and may be used generally to strengthen state departments of education.

All this barely hints at the diverse ways in which the federal government participates in the "local" functioning of primary and secondary education. It does not consider, for example, that employees of the United States Office of Education often serve as officers and leading members of a number of teachers' professional organizations, including the associations whose principal concern is curriculum development in the primary grades. A good portion of the new ideas and new programs that local governments adopt come from these professional groups. A complete catalog of federal aids to education would also have to include the federal government's grants-in-land to states and localities for free public education. This program began in 1785 and, before the public domain was exhausted, supplied some 145 million acres, an area larger than France, for primary and secondary education (excluding the tens of millions of acres recently granted Alaska for the same purposes). So the federal government, through the land grants, was a prime force in making possible the most local of all so-called local functions: free public education.

What is true of education is also true of other functions of American government. Police protection, like education, is considered a uniquely local function. Even more than education, police work involves the continuous collaboration of federal, state, and local authorities, and more recently, formal federal cash grants to aid states and localities in the improvement of law enforcement and criminal justice activities. And the sharing of functions is equally important from the federal perspective. Foreign affairs, national defense, and the development of atomic energy are usually considered to be exclusive responsibilities of the national government. In fact, the state and local governments have extensive responsibilities, directly and indirectly, in each of these fields. The mixture of responsibilities, of course, varies. The federal government, for example, has less to do with fire-fighting than with police protection on the local scene; and the states and localities have less importance in the post office than in atomic energy development. But the larger point is that all areas of American government are involved in all functions.

The federal system is not accurately symbolized by a neat layer cake of three distinct and separate planes. A far more realistic symbol is that of the marble cake. Wherever you slice through it you reveal an inseparable mixture of differently colored ingredients. There is no neat horizontal stratification. Vertical and diagonal lines almost obliterate the horizontal ones, and in some places there are unexpected whirls and an imperceptible merging of colors, so that it is difficult to tell where one ends and the other begins. So it is with federal, state, and local responsibilities in the chaotic marble cake of American government.

## II. Fear of the Federal Octopus:
### Decentralization by Order

The federal system has been criticized in recent years from two sides. On the one hand, it is said that the strength of special and local interests (including the strength of state and local governments) frustrates national policy. In Congress, this critique holds, the power of the peripheries makes consistent national leadership impossible. Members of Congress, dependent for reelection on local constituencies rather than on national centers of party power, can with impunity sacrifice national goals for special interests. This argument concludes that an expansion of national powers is essential. On the other hand, it is said that the power of the national government is growing to such an extent that it threatens to efface the state and local governments, reducing them to compliant administrative arms of national offices. The "federal octopus" is held to threaten the very existence of the states and to destroy local initiative.

The two critiques are to a large extent contradictory. Yet reforms of the federal system are often proposed as if one or the other of these complaints were the complete truth. Those concerned about the federal system are uniformly found expressing fear of the federal octopus.

Four attempts have been made since the end of World War II to strengthen the states by devolving upon them functions now performed by the federal government and we may be into a fifth at the present time. The first and second Hoover Commissions devoted a portion of their energy to this end. The Kestnbaum Commission, although extolling federal-state cooperation in a number of fields,

4

nevertheless operated on the false assumption that "the principal tradition is the tradition of separation." The President's Federal-State Action Committee was established in 1957 at the recommendation of President Eisenhower for the specific purpose of bringing about an ordered devolution of functions from the federal government to the states. It is this last that is especially instructive in light of President Nixon's "New Federalism."

Mr. Eisenhower was greatly concerned over increases in federal functions at the expense of the states, which, he felt, transgress "our most cherished principles of government, and tend to undermine the structure so painstakingly built by those who preceded us." "Those who would stay free," he insisted, "must stand eternal watch against excessive concentration of power in government." The president suggested the formation of a committee, composed of high federal and state officials, whose first mission would be "to designate functions which the States are ready and willing to assume and finance that are now performed or financed wholly or in part by the Federal Government." The president also charged the committee "to recommend the Federal and State revenue adjustments required to enable the States to assume such functions." The effort of the committee, in short, would be to take direct steps against the threat of the federal octopus. The committee would recommend federal functions to be turned over to the states, and would further recommend the transfer of federal tax resources to the states so that they could perform with their own funds the new functions they would assume. "I assure you," Mr. Eisenhower told the governors, "that I wouldn't mind being called a lobbyist for such a worthy cause."[1]

The committee established at Mr. Eisenhower's suggestion was a distinguished one. It had as co-chairmen Robert B. Anderson, secretary of the treasury, and Lane Dwinell, governor of New Hampshire. Two additional cabinet members, as well as the director of the Bureau of the Budget and several members of the president's personal staff, from the federal side, and nine additional governors, from the state side, completed the group. The committee had excel-

---

[1] President Eisenhower's address was delivered before the Governors' Conference on June 24, 1957. For the complete text see Joint Federal-State Action Committee, *Progress Report No. 1* (Washington: U.S. Government Printing Office, 1957), pp. 17–22.

lent staff assistance and complete presidential support. There were no disagreements on party or regional lines. The group was determined not to write just another report, but rather it wished to live up to its name and produce "action" toward decentralization via devolution and separation of functions and tax sources. It worked hard for more than two years.

Never did good intent, hopes, and labor produce such negligible results. The committee could agree on only two activities from which the federal government should withdraw in favor of complete state responsibility. One was the federal grant for sewage-treatment plants; the other was federal aid for vocational education (including aid for practical-nurse training and for training in fishery trades and industry). These programs represented some $80 million of federal funds in 1957, just over 2 percent of all federal grants for that year. To enable the states to finance these functions, the committee recommended a state offset for a fraction of the federal tax on local telephone calls. It was calculated that the offset tax, plus an equalization grant, would provide each state with at least 40 percent more money than it would spend on the two functions it would assume. Some states would receive twice as much.

Faithful to his pledge, President Eisenhower recommended all aspects of this program to Congress. Opposition devolepd from those benefiting from the vocational-education and sewage-plant grants. Many individual mayors, the American Municipal Association, the United States Conference of Mayors, the several professional groups concerned with vocational education, public health and sportsmen's association, state departments of education, and even a large number of governors were included in the opposition. As modest as the program was and as generous as the financing provisions seemed to be, no part of the recommendations was made law. The entire program died before the end of Eisenhower's presidency. Indeed, both programs have since been expanded substantially.

### III. The Failure to Decentralize by Order

Why have all attempts to decentralize the federal system failed? Why has it proved impossible to separate federal and state functions by an act of the national government?

6

# The American Federal System

In the first place, the history of the American governments is a history of shared functions. All nostalgic references to the days of state and local independence are based upon mythical views of the past. There has in fact never been a time when federal, state, and local functions were separate and distinct. Government does more things in 1974 than it did in 1790 or 1861; but in terms of what government did, there was as much sharing of functions then as today. The effort to decentralize government through the ordered separation of functions is contrary to 180 years of experience.[2]

### THE NATURE OF AMERICAN POLITICS

A second reason for the failure to decentralize government by order is inherent in the nature of American political parties. The political parties of this country are themselves highly decentralized. They respond to directives from bottom to top, rather than from top to bottom. Except during periods of crisis, not even the president of the United States requesting action from a congressman or senator can command the sort of accommodating response that, as a matter of course, follows requests from an individual, an interest group, or a mayor of a city in the legislator's district. The legislator, of course, cannot fully meet all constituent requests; indeed, their very multiplicity, and their frequently conflicting character, are a liberating force, leaving room for individual judgment, discretion, and the expression of conviction. Nevertheless, the orientation of the vast majority of congressmen and senators is toward constituency. Constituency, not party or president, is principally responsible for the legislator's election and reelection. And he feels that accommodation to his constituency, rather than to party leaders, is his principal obligation.

The parties are thus not at all, as they are in other countries, centralizing forces. On the contrary, they act to disperse power. And the significant point here is that they disperse power in favor of state and local governments.

[2] See Daniel J. Elazar, *The American Partnership: Intergovernmental Cooperation in the Nineteenth Century United States* (Chicago: University of Chicago Press, 1962).

# Morton Grodzins and Daniel Elazar

I have described the actual mechanisms in another place.[3] Briefly, the parties can be seen as decentralizers in four ways. (1) They make possible the "multiple crack" attribute of American politics. That is to say, the loose party arrangements provide innumerable access points through which individuals, interest groups, and local and state governments take action to influence the processes of national legislation and administration. (2) The party arrangements are responsible for giving to state governments a role in national programs. What is remarkable in recent history is how consistently the Congress has insisted that the states, and now the localities, share responsibility in programs that, from constitutional and administrative considerations, might easily have been all-national programs. The local orientation of the members of Congress, overriding the desires of national party leaders, is clearly responsible for this phenomenon. (3) The party system also makes possible the widespread, institutionalized interference of members of Congress in national administrative programs on behalf of local constituents (again including the state and local governments). This, on The Hill, is called "case work." The bureaucracy in the United States is subject to an hour-by-hour scrutiny by members of the Congress. No aspect of procedure and no point of policy is free from inquiry. Any administrative decision made in a national agency that is contrary, for example, to the desire of a mayor or governor is immediately subject to congressional inquiry which, if not satisfactorily answered, can in the end produce a meeting in a cabinet member's office, or a full-scale congressional investigation, or a threat of reprisal through the appropriation or legislative process. (4) Finally, the loose national parties, since they cannot themselves supply the political support needed by administrators of national agencies, force administrators to seek their own support in Congress. This support must come from locally oriented members of the Congress. The result is that national administrative policies must be made with great sensitivity to the desires of state and local governments and other local interests.

What does this have to do with decentralization by order? There can be no such decentralization as long as the president cannot control a majority of the Congress, and he can rarely exercise

[3] "American Political Parties and the American System," *Western Political Quarterly*, Vol. XIII (December, 1960), pp. 974–98.

this control, as long as the parties remain in their decentralized state. The decentralization of parties indicates a decentralization of power that is strong enough to prevent a presidentially sponsored decentralization of government. States and localities, working through the parties, can assume that they will have an important role in many national programs; that is to say, there will be few domestic all-federal programs. The parties also give the peripheral governments significant influence in the administration of national programs, including those in which they have no formal role.

Influence of the federal government in state and local operations, made possible by its purse power and exercised through grants-in-aid, is more than balanced by the political power of the peripheral units, exercised through the multiple crack, the localism of legislators, their "case work," and the political role of federal administrators. Politics here are stronger than the purse, in part because the locally oriented Congress is also the final arbiter of federal expenditures. The states and localities are more influential in federal affairs than the federal government is in theirs. And this influence must be a part of the equation when balancing the strength of state and local governments against the national government. State and local officials, whatever their verbally expressd opposition to centralization, do not in fact find federal activities a threat to their position because of their substantial control over those activities.

In sum, the nation's politics, misunderstood by those advocating decentralization by order, accounts in large part for the failure to achieve that sort of decentralization.

### THE DIFFICULTY OF DIVIDING FUNCTIONS:
### THE ISSUE OF "CLOSENESS"

History and politics are two reasons for the failure of decentralization by order. A third, related, reason is the sheer difficulty of dividing functions between central and peripheral units without the division resulting in further centralization.

It is often claimed that local or state governments are "closer" to the people than the federal government, and are therefore the preferred instrument for public action. If one carefully examines this statement, it proves to be quite meaningless.

"Closeness" when applied to governments means many things.

## Morton Grodzins and Daniel Elazar

One meaning is the provision of services directly to the people. Another meaning is participation. A third is control: to say that local governments are closer to the people than the federal government is to say that citizens can control the former more easily and more completely than the latter. A fourth meaning is understanding, a fifth communication, a sixth identification. Thorough analysis of "closeness" would have to compare local, state, and federal governments with respect to all these, as well as other, meanings of the term.

Such an analysis reveals that in few, if any, of these meanings are the state and local units "closer" to the people than the federal governments. The big differences are between rural or small urban communities on the one hand and the big cities on the other: citizens in the former are "closer" (in many, but not all, meanings) to both the local and federal governments than are residents of big urban areas.

Consider, for example, "closeness" as the provision of services. All governments in the American system operate in direct contact with people at their places of residence and work, and in important activities the units operate collaboratively. It cannot even be said that the local units provide the most important local services. The important services are those of shared responsibility. Where it is possible to recognize primary responsibilities, the greater importance of local government does not at all emerge.

Where in the American system is the government closest to the people as a provider of services? The answer is clearly neither the local nor federal government in urban areas and not even local government in rural areas. Rather it is the federal government in rural areas that is closest to the people (as a provider of services). As a consumer of services the farmer has more governmental wares to cl oose from than any other citizen. They are largely federal or federally sponsored wares, and they cover virtually all aspects of his personal and economic life.

If he wished to take full advantage of what was offered, an individual farmer could assemble a veritable convention of government helpers in his home and fields. He could have a soil-conservation technician make a survey of his property, prepare plans for conservation practices and watershed protection, and give advice on crops, growing practices, wood-lot plantings, and wild-life maintenance. A Forest Service officer collaboratively with a state forester would provide low-cost tree stock. Extension workers would aid the farmer's wife on all aspects of home management, including gardening, cooking, and sewing; instruct the children with respect to a whole range of health, recreational, and agricultural problems; provide the farmer himself with demonstrations and information aimed at reducing costs, increasing income, and adjusting production to market demands, and give the entire family instruction with respect to "social relations, adjustments and cultural values." An officer of the Agricultural Conservation Program would arrange federal grants for part of the costs of his soil and conservation practices, including ditching and building ponds. (Another official would provide a supply of fish at little or no cost with which to stock the pond.) A Commodity Stabilization Service worker would arrange for loans on some crops, for government purchase of others, and for special incentive payments on still a third category: he would also pay the farmer for constructing crop-storage facilities. Another officer from the same agency would arrange cash payments to the farmer under the soil-bank program, if he takes out of production acres devoted to designated basic crops (the "acreage reserve") or puts general cropland to conservation use (the "conservation reserve"). An official of the Farmers Home Administration, if credit is not elsewhere available, will make loans to the farmer for the operation, improvement, and enlargement of his property, and (to maximize repayment possibilities) will "service" the farmer-borrower by providing him with comprehensive and continuous technical advice on how to make his operation as profitable as possible. All this just begins the list.

It can be concluded that the farm sector of the population receives a wider range of governmental services than any other population group. These services are largely inspired by federal legislation and largely financed with federal funds. From the point of view of services rendered, the federal government is clearly "closest" to the farm population and closer to it than any other American government is to the population it serves. Outside of institutionalized persons and those dependent upon relief, the American farmer receives at first hand more governmental services than any other American.

And while he receives these services as the consequence of collaboration among all governments, the federal government plays the key role.

Local rural governments (but not local urban ones) show to better advantage when closeness as participation is considered. Only if participation is measured in terms of voting do the local rural units rank low. Elections for national offices almost invariably turn out a larger fraction of the eligible voters than local elections. And rural local elections attract proportionately fewer voters than urban local elections. Voting aside, participation in rural, local governments possesses an intensity and personal quality that is, on the whole, unmatched for other governments. In part, this participation is the consequence of simple arithmetic. Where relatively many governments serve relatively few people, participation of citizens in some ways must increase. Pure statistical chance will produce a large fraction of rural residents—and their relatives, neighbors, and friends—who are elected or appointed to public office. Governmental services become hand tooled under such circumstances. Recipients of services personally share in the decisions of government, and the services themselves become personalized. A father, for example, will deliver his son to jail, explaining to his neighbor, the chief of police, that the lad has been drinking and that the family would appreciate the courtesy of allowing him to spend a few days in safety behind bars. Poor relief is granted when a doctor telephones a country supervisor who then walks across the street to talk to the welfare officer. A farmer can appear personally before his neighbors on the township or county board to argue that an old road near his place should be scraped or a new one built. A township meeting may be adjourned so that a person arguing his case for a new drainage ditch can go home to his chores before dark. I have visited a mayor being consulted in his hardware store by parents complaining about a dangerous school crossing; and I have attended traffic court in the blueberry patch of the justice of the peace

This sort of community government—of neighbors serving neighbors in a neighborly fashion—has not been (and perhaps cannot be) duplicated in the big cities (although urban surrogates are sought and achieved in some measure by political organizations and, more recently, by community action groups stimulated by federal anti-poverty programs). The federal government in rural areas—through its extensive network of local units—is in many ways similar to rural local governments in these marks of closeness via participation. So are some suburban governments. But no big city government as presently structured can achieve the attributes of neighborly participation found widely in the rural areas. If "closeness" is participation, therefore, rural local governments—followed by rural federal government in its several forms—achieve levels and styles of closeness unattainable in urban areas. The important partial exception for rural local governments is participation in voting.

Closeness as participation should not be confused with closeness as control. Indeed, maximum citizen participation may be combined with maximum control in the hands of a minority. In general there is no evidence that residents of rural areas direct the affairs of their local governments to a greater extent than the big-city dwellers. In several significant ways, they have less control over the governments serving them.

Rural local governments are probably more frequently boss-controlled than any other American governments. Roscoe C. Martin has said flatly that local rural government is "too small to be truly democratic."[4] He referred particularly to the fact that these governments did not excite or stimulate citizens and that the scope of rural governments was "too picayune, too narrow in outlook, too limited in horizon, too self-centered in interests...." Beyond such considerations, in small communities homogeneity of outlook may be combined with gross inequality of power. A small group of farmers or businessmen, a single politician, or a rich family of old settlers can frequently control the entire politics of a rural community. The control may contain attributes of beneficence, and it may be wielded silently. It nevertheless represents an effective monopolization of power over those things that the rural government does and refuses to do. The small size of the community means that minority groups find difficulty in organizing opposition, a difficulty that is compounded by the wide range of personal, social, and economic penalities that may be exacted by the ruling group. The widespread sharing of influence is not impossible in the small community; but

[4] *Grass Roots* (University: University of Alabama Press, 1957), p. 92.

possibilities of clique and one-man rule are maximized, ideal images of small-town democracy notwithstanding.[5]

A system of shared governmental functions by its very nature rarely allows a single government to exercise complete control over a given activity. All officers of government in the United States consequently experience what may be called "frustration of scope of action." This is the frustration produced by the inability of decision-makers in one government to produce action at their own discretion: other governments must also be moved. Limited scope of discretion is felt universally, by the largest as well as the smallest governments, but it is felt most keenly by the rural local governments.

The smaller the government, the more limited the span of control. Hardly any function of the small rural government does not involve other governments. A farmer may gain full support from local officers with respect to where a road should go through his land, but he sees the road go elsewhere because the basic decisions are not made by his friends in the local government but by the combined efforts of local, county, state, and federal officials. Decisions of rural governments with respect to most other matters are similarly conditioned by decision-makers elsewhere. Frustration of scope of control, if a universal of the American system, is nevertheless felt most acutely in the small local governments of rural America.

Channels exist by which local populations can bring effective pressure to bear upon officers of the state and federal governments. Sharing by local groups in the decisions of those governments is characteristic. But this sort of influence is not the consequence of the opportunity of rural citizens to participate actively and directly in their governments. Rather it is the consequence of the form and operation of American political parties. Similarly, the considerable rural control of federal agricultural programs is not the result of farmer participation in the many federally sponsored local governments. In this case, direct participation at the grass roots may be only a shadow of genuine power and may indeed be a device of

[5] A prime example of a rural political boss emerges from the pages of Arthur J. Vidich and Joseph Bensman, *Small Town in Mass Society* (Princeton: Princeton University Press, 1958).

others to implement their own programs. We are discovering that this is equally true in the big city anti-poverty programs with all their emphasis on citizen participation. Unremitting civic participation is more characteristic of totalitarianism than of democracy, and the greater participation of rural over urban citizens in the affairs of local governments cannot be equated with the citizen control of those governments.

The full analysis of all meanings of closeness would not establish that local governments are in significant ways "closest" to the people. Only a portion of the analysis has been presented here. Incomplete as it is, it is sufficient to demonstrate that the criteria of closeness cannot serve to give more functions to local governments.

### THE DIFFICULTY OF DIVIDING FUNCTIONS:
#### ISSUES OF LOGIC

Nor does it help, on grounds of logic, to attempt a division of federal and state (or local) functions. Indeed, such a division would probably result in putting virtually all functions in the hands of the national government.

The logical difficulty of dividing functions can be seen in the Federal-State Action Committee's recommendation for turning over all responsibility for constructing sewage plants to the states and localities. The committee's reason for recommending this program, rather than others, was only a simple affirmation:

> The Joint Federal-State Action Committee holds that local waste-treatment facilities are primarily a local concern and their construction should be primarily a local or State financial responsibility. . . . There is no evidence to demonstrate the continuing need for the present Federal subsidy of an essentially local responsibility.[6]

This sort of language was necessary because no more reasoned argument was possible. There is no way to distinguish, for example, the "localness" of sewage-treatment plants from the "nationalness" of, say, grants for public health. Both programs are equally aimed

[6] *Progress Report No. 1* (December, 1957), p. 6.

at increasing public health and safety. Where there are no adequate plants, the untreated sewage creates health hazards, including higher infant-mortality rates. This sewage, when dumped into streams (the usual practice), creates in many cases interstate hazards to health and safety. Every indicator of "localness" attributed to sewage-treatment plants can also be attributed to public-health programs. And every attribute of "nationalness" in one is also found in the other. Barely ten years after the committee's report, it was difficult to find any knowledgeable people who were prepared to argue that sewage-treatment was simply a local matter.

Why did the committee choose sewage plants—rather than public-health grants, or federal old-age assistance, or the federal school-milk program—to transfer to states and localities? Clearly not because one program is more "local" than the other. The real basis of choice can be easily guessed. The federal sewage-plant program was relatively new, and it did not have as many direct recipients of aid as the other programs. The political risk to the governors of recommending local responsibility for sewage-treatment plants was relatively small. To recommend federal withdrawal from public health, or old-age assistance, or the school-lunch program would have aroused the wrath of numerous individuals and interest groups. Governors cannot alienate such groups and still remain governors. The choice of sewage-treatment plants as "primarily a local concern" had little or nothing to do with genuine distinctions between local and national functions.

A detailed analysis would show that any division of functions, on the line of their "local" or "national" character, would leave precious few activities in the local category. In 1963, automobile safety, for example, was almost exclusively a state and local (and private) responsibility. Although automobile deaths approached 40,000 annually, the injuries exceeded 1,500,000. If the number of deaths due to road accidents in even a small state were the result of an airplane crash, several teams of federal officers, operating under a number of federal statutes, would have been combing the area in order to prevent further deaths. But there were no federal officers on the scene to prevent further auto deaths, not even if some fatalities in California were caused by drivers licensed in New York. In a division of responsibilities, assuming that they have to be all federal or all state-local, would automobile safety have remained in the state-local category? As it was, only a few years later, in response to certain public pressures, the federal government did enter the automobile safety field with serious intent but it did so in a manner that reflected the federal nature of the body politics, assuming major direct responsibilities for setting the safety standards of vehicles while requiring (and bribing) the states to enforce minimum federal standards (or better) on the road themselves. There are still no federal officers at each crash scene but the problem itself is being treated "federally."

This sort of analysis can be applied to a number of fields in which states and localities have important, if not exclusive, responsibility. It is hard to find any area in which the states and localities would remain in control, if a firm division of functions were to take place. Not even education would be an exception. Pseudo-historical considerations, outworn conceptions of "closeness," and fears of an American brand of totalitarianism would argue for an exclusive state-local control of primary and secondary education. But inequities of state resources, disparities in educational facilities and results, the gap between actual and potential educational services, and, above all, the adverse national consequences that might follow long-term inadequacies of state-local control would almost certainly, if the choice had to be made, establish education as the exclusive concern of the national government.

The clear conclusion is that widespread separation of functions would reduce states and localities to institutions of utter unimportance. They can no longer sustain the claim that they are closer to the people. Their strength has never been a strength of isolation. Their future depends upon their continued ability to assume important roles in the widening scope of public service and regulation. Their future, in short, depends upon the continuation of shared responsibilities in the American federal system.

## IV. Decentralization via Strengthening of State Governments

The strength of state governments is not often measured in terms of the states' influence on national programs. Rather the strength of the states is most frequently discussed as state independence, or at least as fiscal and administrative power sufficient to carry out their own functions. It is often held that federal programs follow the failure of the states to meet their own responsibilities. "By using their power to strengthen their own governments and those of their subdivisions," the Kestnbaum Commission said, "the States can relieve much of the pressure for, and generate a strong counterpressure against, improper expansion of National action."[7] A distinguished scholar of American politics, V. O. Key, has expressed the same point, although somewhat more guardedly. He considers deficiencies of representation in state legislatures, constitutional restrictions on state power, and state political systems as a "centralizing factor in the federal system."

> Evidently the organization of state politics builds into the governmental system a more or less purely political factor that contributes to federal centralization. The combination of party system and the structure of representation in most of the states incapacitates the states and diverts demands for political action to Washington.[8]

The argument's simplicity is persuasive. But what it accurately describes is insignificant, and for larger events it is wrong. The inability of state legislatures and executives to plan a national airport program undoubtedly led to federal grants in that field. But could the states, even if endowed with ideal constitutions, legislatures, and political parties, be expected to design and finance such a program? The same sort of question could be asked with respect to housing and urban renewal, the second conspicuous federal-local program of the postwar era. (In both fields, incidentally, the states are given the chance to assume important responsibilities and an increasing number do so.) The great expansion of federal domestic programs came during the depression. Certainly it can be said that the federal government went into the business of welfare on a wholesale scale because the states were unable to do the job. Was state inability the result of the ineffectiveness of state political parties, inequities of

---

[7] The Commission on Intergovernmental Relations, *A Report to the President* (Washington: Government Printing Office, 1955), p. 56.

[8] *American State Politics* (New York: Alfred A. Knopf, 1956), pp. 81, 266–67.

legislative representation, and outmoded constitutions? Or was the states' inability the result of a catastrophic depression? The first factors may have had some effect, but they are picayune compared with the devastating impact of the depression on state income. And the depression would have demanded action from the federal government (with its virtually unlimited borrowing power) in new fields whatever the status of the states' political parties or the modernity of their constitutional arrangement.

Furthermore, expansion of national programs has not only followed the *failure* of state programs; the nation has also assumed responsibility upon demonstration of the *success* of state programs. Thus requirements for health and safety in mining and manufacturing, the maintenance of minimum wages, unemployment compensation, aid to the aged and blind, and even the building of roads, were all undertaken, more or less successfully, by some or even most states before they were assumed as national functions. So the states can lose exclusive functions both ways. The national government steps in as an emulator when the states produce useful innovations, making national programs of state successes; and it steps in when crisis is created as the consequence of state failure, making national programs of state inadequacies.

The role of the national government as an emulator is fostered by the nationwide communication network and the nationwide political process which produce public demands for national minimum standards. The achievement of such standards in some states raises the issue of reaching them in all. Many reasons exist for this tendency: for example, the citizens of the active states feel that with their higher tax rates they are pricing themselves out of the market. Those in the laggard states can find specific points of comparison to demonstrate that their services are unsatisfactory. National fiscal aid may be essential for the economically disadvantaged states. State legislatures may be less congenial to a given program than the national Congress. Combinations of these and other causes mean that national programs will continue to come into being although, and even because, some states carry out those programs with high standards. The only way to avoid this sort of expansion by the national government would be if all fifty states were politically, fiscally, and administratively able to undertake, more or less simultaneously, a given program at acceptable national standards. This is not likely to happen. Even if it were, those in states less likely to undertake the program are certain to raise public demands for the national government to take responsibility for it.

If both state failures and state successes produce national programs, it must be added that neither of those mechanisms is the important cause for the expansion of the central government. This expansion, in largest part, has been produced by the dangers of the twentieth century. (War, defense, and related items constitute more than 70 percent of the federal budget, and federal increases of non-defense activities lag far behind expenditure increases by the states and localities.) National-security items aside, the free votes of a free people have sustained federal programs in such areas as public welfare, highway, airports, hospitals and public health, agriculture, schools, and housing and urban redevelopment, to name only some of the largest grant-in-aid programs. The plain fact is that large population groups are better represented in the constituencies of the president and Congress than they are in the constituencies of governors and state legislatures. No realistic program of erasing inequities of representation in state legislatures—not even action consequent to the Supreme Court's reapportionment decision—will significantly alter this fact in the foreseeable future. Only those who hold that "the federal government is something to be feared" (to use the words of Senator Morse, in his minority criticism of the Kestnbaum Commission Report) would wish to make the federal government unresponsive to those national needs expressed through the democratic process, needs which by their very nature will not, and cannot, be met by state action.

In sum, strong as well as weak states turn "demands for political action to Washington." More important, the ability of the national government to meet citizen needs that cannot be met by either strong or weak states, whatever those adjectives mean, also accounts for the expansion (as well as for the very existence) of the federal government. Strengthening states, in the sense of building more effective parties and of providing legislatures and executives who have a readiness and capacity for action, may indeed prevent an occasional program from being taken up by the federal government. The total possible effect can only be insignificant. The only way

# The American Federal System

to produce a significant decline in federal programs, new and old, would be to induce citizens to demand fewer activities from all governments. (The cry, "Strengthen the states," in many cases only means, "Decrease all governmental activity.") This is an unlikely development in an age of universal literacy, quick communications, and heightened sensitivities to material factors in the good life, as well as to the political appeals of an alternative political system. One can conclude that strengthening the states so that they can perform independent functions and thereby prevent federal expansion is a project that cannot succeed.

Historical trend lines, the impetus of technology, and the demands of citizenry are all in the direction of central action. The wonder is not that the central government has done so much, but rather that it has done so little. The parties, reflecting the nation's social structure, have at once slowed up centralization and given the states (and localities) important responsibilities in central government programs. Furthermore, political strength is no fixed quantum. Increasing one institution's power need not decrease the power of another in the same system. Indeed, the centralization that has taken place in the United States has also strengthened the states— with respect to personnel practices, budgeting, the governors' power, citizens' interest, and the scope of state action—as every impartial study of federal aid has shown.[9] The states remain strong and active forces in the federal system. The important reason that state institutions should be further strengthened is so that they may become more effective innovators and even stronger partners in a governmental system of shared responsibilities.

## V. Two Kinds of Decentralization

If I have not proved, I hope I have at least given reasonable grounds for believing: First, the American federal system is principally characterized by a federal-state-local sharing of responsibilities for virtually all functions. Second, our history and politics in largest

[9] See, for example, *The Impact of Federal Grants-in-Aid on the Structure and Functions of State and Local Governments* (a study covering 25 states submitted to the Commission on Intergovernmental Relations), by the Governmental Affairs Institute (Washington, 1955); and the report of the New York Temporary Commission on the Fiscal Affairs of State Government (the Bird Commission) (Albany, 1955), especially Vol. II, pp. 431–672.

part account for this sharing. Third, there is no reasonable possibility of dividing functions between the federal government, on the one hand, and states and localities, on the other, without drastically reducing the importance of the latter. Fourth, no "strengthening" of state or local (or neighborhood) governments will materially reduce the present functions of the federal government; nor will it have any marked effect on the rate of acquisition of new federal functions.

A final point may now be made. Those who attempt to decentralize by order are far more likely to produce centralization by order. In so doing they will destroy the decentralization already existing in the United States. Therein lies much of the paradox of Mr. Nixon's recent proposals to "improve" the operation of the federal system, which, to date, have led to an expansion of the federal role rather than its contraction in any respect.

The circumstances making possible a decentralization by a decision of central officials are simple to specify. What is principally needed is a president and a congressional majority of the same party, the president consistently able to command a majority of the Congress through the control of his party. With such an arrangement, a recommendation by a committee of cabinet members and governors or some other body to devolve functions to the states and localities if strongly backed by the president, could be readily implemented. Party control of the central government and the president's control of Congress through his party are the essentials. In other words, party *centralization* must precede governmental *decentralization by order*.

But a centralized party pledged to decentralization—to minimizing central government activities—can hardly be or remain a majority party in the twentieth century. The power to decentralize by order must, by its very nature, also be the power to centralize by order. Centralized majority parties are far more likely to choose in favor of centralization than decentralization.

Decentralization by order must be contrasted with another sort of decentralization. This is the decentralization that exists as the result of independent centers of power and that operates through the chaos of American political processes and political institutions. It may be called decentralization by mild chaos. It is less tidy and noisier than an ordered decentralization. But it is not dependent upon action of central bodies, and its existence is not at the mercy of changing parties or of changing party policy.

If decentralization is a desirable end, decentralization by mild chaos is far preferable to decentralization by order. The former is built upon genuine points of political strength. It is more permanent. And, most important, it is a decentralization of genuinely shared power, as well as of shared functions. Decentralization by order might maintain a sharing of functions, but it cannot, because of its nature, maintain a sharing of political power. An ordered decentralization depends upon a central power which, by the very act of ordering decentralization, must drastically diminish, if not obliterate, the political power of the peripheral units of government.

A president of the United States at present does not have consistent control of his Congress. The power of the president is often contested by the power of individuals, interest groups, and states and localities, made manifest through the undisciplined parties. And the president is not always the winner. President Eisenhower was not the winner in his proposals to devolve federal functions to the states. (His situation was complicated by the fact that his party was a minority of the Congress, but the results would almost certainly have been the same if he had had a majority.) He lost because his proposals were contested by many governors, many mayors, their professional organizations, and a number of other groups. The party system allowed these protests to be elevated over the decision of the president. Today Mr. Nixon is in an extraordinarily similar position.

Thus the strength of states and localities in the federal system is evidenced in the failure to decentralize by order. Successful decentralization by order would mean the decline of state and local power and the death of America's undisciplined parties. It could only follow profound changes in the nation's political style and supporting social structure.

The rhetoric of state and national power becomes easily and falsely a rhetoric of conflict. It erroneously conceives states and localities, on one side, and the central government, on the other, as adversaries. There are undoubtedly occasions when the advantage of a locality, state, or region is a disadvantage to the nation as a whole. But in most circumstances at most times compatibility rather than conflict of interests is characteristic. There are sufficient, if often overlooked, reasons for this compatibility. The nation's diversities exist within a larger unity. Voters at local, state, and national elections are the same voters. A congressman in one role is a local citizen in another. Professional workers in education, welfare, health, road-building and other fields adhere to the same standards of achievement, regardless of which government pays their salaries. Federal, state, and local officials are not adversaries. They are colleagues. The sharing of functions and powers is impossible without a whole. The American system is best conceived as one government serving one people.

MARTIN DIAMOND

•

# WHAT THE FRAMERS MEANT BY
# FEDERALISM*

With us the Founding Fathers have great authority. The Constitution they framed is our fundamental legal document. The worthiness of their work has rightly earned from us a profound respect for their political wisdom. The Founding Fathers therefore have for us the combined authority of law and wisdom, a very great authority indeed. But to pay our respect to that authority—to know how to obey intelligently or, sometimes, when and how to differ intelligently— we must know precisely what their Constitution meant and the political thought of which it is the legal expression. "What you have inherited from your fathers/You must first earn to make your own." Ours is such a patrimony that its possession requires constant recovery by careful study.

We are fortunate that we have in our possession a sufficient, objective basis for an understanding of the Framers. Six writings tell nearly the whole story: the Declaration of Independence, the Articles of Confederation, the proceedings of the Federal Convention, the Constitution, *The Federalist,* and the anti-Federalist essays. The Declaration is the primeval statement of our political principles. The Articles were the "constitution" that was rejected. The proceedings are the extraordinary record of the way the Constitution was put together. The Constitution is our fundamental law. *The Federalist* is the brilliant and authoritative exposition of the meaning and intention of the Constitution. The anti-Federalist essays are the thoughtful defense of the political tradition the Constitution

* This paper was written while the author was enjoying a fellowship year at the Center for Advanced Study in the Behavioral Sciences.

was displacing. These are, as it were, the simple stock of the patrimony, available to all.

These writings must be carefully mined and made to yield up the political principles upon which our system rests. Surprisingly, little has been done with the principle for which our system has been most famous—federalism. Relatively little serious attention has been given to the Framers' own view of federalism, because something confidently called "modern federalism" has been understood to have superseded the original version. It is the contention of this essay that the recovery of the Framers' view of federalism is necessary to the understanding of American federalism. In what follows, an attempt is made to indicate what the Framers meant by federalism, as that is revealed in the proceedings of the Federal Convention.

## I

The American Republic has been regarded by nearly all modern observers as *the* example of a federal government. Indeed the various modern definitions of federalism are little more than slightly generalized descriptions of the American way of governing:

> Federalism may be defined as the division of political power between a central government, with authority over the entire territory of a nation, and a series of local governments, called 'states' in America. . . .[1]
>
> A federation is a single state in which the powers and functions of government are divided between a central government and several "local" governments, each having a sphere of jurisdiction within which it is supreme.[2]
>
> The essential relationship involves a division of activities between the autonomous parts and the common or central organs of a composite whole.[3]

According to these typical definitions, the essential federal characteristic is the "division of political power," a division of supremacy (sovereignty, as used to be said) between member states

---

[1] Carr, Bernstein, Morrison, Snyder, McLean, *American Democracy in Theory and Practice* (rev. ed.; New York: Rinehart and Co., 1955), p. 78.
[2] Holloway and Ader, *American Government* (New York: The Ronald Press Co., 1959), p. 13.
[3] Professor A. W. Macmahon's article on "Federalism" in *Encyclopedia of the Social Sciences* (New York: Macmillan, 1937), VI, 173.

# What the Framers Meant by Federalism

and a central government, each having the final say regarding matters belonging to its sphere. There is a corollary to this sort of definition which has also come to be generally accepted. All college students are now taught that, in this respect, there are three kinds of government—confederal, federal, and unitary (national)—and that the United States exemplifies the middle term. This familiar distinction illuminates the definitions of federalism. In this view, a confederacy and a nation are seen as the extremes. The defining characteristic of a confederacy is that the associated states retain all the sovereign power, with the central body entirely dependent legally upon their will; the defining characteristic of a nation is that the central body has all the sovereign power, with the localities entirely dependent legally upon the will of the nation. In this view, then, federalism is truly the middle term, for its defining characteristic is that it modifies and then combines the best characteristics of the other two forms. A *federal* system combines states which *confederally* retain sovereignty within a certain sphere, with a central body that *nationally* possesses sovereignty within another sphere; the combination is thought to create a new and better thing to which is given the name federalism.

Now what is strange is this. The leading Framers viewed their handiwork in an entirely different light. For example, *The Federalist,* the great contemporary exposition of the Constitution, emphatically does not regard the Constitution as establishing a typically federal, perhaps not even a primarily federal system of government. *The Federalist* regards the new American Union as departing significantly from the essentially federal character. The decisive statement is: "The proposed Constitution, therefore, is, in strictness, neither a national nor a federal Constitution, but a composition of both."[4] As will become clear, our now familiar tripartite distinction was completely unknown to the men who made the Constitution. They had a very different understanding than we do of what federalism is. For them, there were but two possible modes: confederal or federal as opposed to unitary or national. They had, therefore, in strictness, to regard their Constitution as a composition of federal and national features. We now give the single word federal to the

---

[4] *Federalist* 39, p. 250. All references are to the edition of Henry Cabot Lodge, introduction by Edward Mead Earle (New York: Modern Library, 1941).

# Martin Diamond

system the Framers regarded as possessing both federal and national features. This means we now regard as a unique principle what they regarded as a mere compound.

Consider Tocqueville's opinion: "Evidently this is no longer a federal government, but an incomplete national government, which is neither exactly national nor exactly federal; but the new word which ought to express this novel thing does not yet exist."[5] For good or ill, the word which came to express the novel thing turned out to be the old word federal. It is no fussy antiquarianism to assert the necessity to understand the Constitution the way its creators did, as possessing both federal and national features. In order to understand the system they created for us and how they expected it to work, we must be able to distinguish the parts that make up the whole, and see the peculiar place of each part in the working of the whole. Now they regarded certain parts as federal and certain parts as national, and had different expectations regarding each. To use the word federal, as we do now, to describe both the "federal" and "national" features of their plan is to lump under one obscuring term things they regarded as radically different. It becomes thus difficult if not impossible to understand their precise intentions. This is a sufficient reason to do the job of recovering precisely what they meant by federalism.

Federalism meant then exactly what we mean now by confederalism: "a sort of association or league of sovereign states." Consider the following from the contemporary dictionary:

Federal . . . from foedus (faith) . . . Relating to a
  league or contract.
Federacy . . . a confederate.
Federation . . . a League.
Federative . . . Having power to make a league or contract.[6]

[5] *Democracy in America,* ed. Phillips Bradley (New York: Alfred A. Knopf, 1945), I, 159.
[6] Samuel Johnson's *Dictionary of the English Language* (2 vols.; Heidelberg: Joseph Englemann, 1828). See also John Walker's *Pronouncing Dictionary and Expositor of the English Language* (Philadelphia: Ambrose Walker, 1818). (The pre-1787 editions do not differ from the later editions here quoted.) Note also Johnson's following definitions. "Confederacy . . . A league; a contract by which several persons engage to support each other; federal compact. . . . Confederate . . . To league; to unite in a league. . . . Confederation . . . League; alliance."

28

## What the Framers Meant by Federalism

In short, the single thing, federalism or confederalism, was characterized by a contractual, voluntary relationship of states and had therefore the status of a league. A brief consideration of the Articles of Confederation will further reveal what men meant then by a federal arrangement, especially when comparison is made to the Constitution.

In recent years we have come to think of the Articles as having created too weak a central government. This is not precise enough. Strictly speaking, neither the friends nor the enemies of the Confederation regarded the Articles as having created any kind of *government* at all, weak or otherwise. Article III declared that "the said states hereby enter into a firm *league of friendship* with each other." Again the contemporary dictionary is helpful.

> League . . . A confederacy; a combination either of interest
> or friendship.
> To League . . . To unite on certain terms; to confederate.

Men referred then to the Articles as a kind of treaty, and, no more than any other treaty organization is thought to create a government, was it thought that the Articles had created one. The language of the Articles makes this clear. The word government never appears in that document, whereas the Constitution speaks repeatedly of the Government, the Treasury, the Authority, the Offices, the Laws of the United States. There are no such terms in the Articles; there could be none because it was fatally a federal arrangement, a league not a government.

Article I declared that "the stile of this confederacy shall be 'The United States of America.'" Twice more at the outset that capitalized expression occurs. But on every subsequent occasion (about forty times) the term is given in lower case letters as the "united states." That is, as a mere league, the Confederacy was not a governmental being to which a proper name could be strictly applied. In the Constitution, on the contrary, the term United States is invariably capitalized. Indeed, the formal language of the Articles makes clear that the Confederacy had no real existence save when the states were formally assembled. When speaking of its duties or functions, the Articles invariably refer to the Confederacy as "the united states *in Congress assembled.*" All men seem to have referred to the Confederacy in this exact phrase. It must be remembered also that the word "Congress" did not then mean an institution of government. As an ordinary word it meant then simply a "meeting," especially "an assembly of envoys, commissioners, deputies, etc. from different courts, meeting to agree on terms of political accommodation."[7] Under the Articles the United States had no being; its existence consisted solely in the congregation of envoys from the separate states for the accommodation of certain specified matters under terms prescribed by the federal treaty. The slightest glance at the Constitution, of course, shows that it refers to the duties and powers of the government of a country.

The Founding Fathers, like all other men at the time and perhaps all other men up to that time, regarded federalism, not as a kind of government, but as a voluntary association of states who sought certain advantages from that association. For example, at the very outset of the Convention, it became necessary for the delegates to state openly their understanding of the nature of the federal form. Gouverneur Morris "explained the distinction between a *federal* and *national, supreme* government; the former being a mere compact resting on the good faith of the parties; the latter having a complete and *compulsive* operation."[8] The entire Convention, with the single exception of Hamilton, in one remark, concurred in this view of the nature of federalism.[9]

From this view it followed that any federal arrangement would be characterized by certain ways of doing things. As one delegate put it, "a confederacy supposes sovereignty in the members composing it and sovereignty supposes equality."[10] That is, when forming a league, the member states retain their political character, i.e., sovereignty; and, each being equally a political entity, each state participates in the league as an equal member. That is, each state has one equal vote in making the league's decisions; moreover, because the league is a voluntary association of sovereign states and

[7] Johnson, *Dictionary. . . .*
[8] *Documents Illustrative of the Formation of the Union of the American States,* ed. C. C. Tansill (Washington: U.S. Government Printing Office, 1927), p. 121. Italics supplied.
[9] *Ibid.,* p. 216.
[10] *Ibid.,* p. 182.

rests upon the "good faith" of the members, extraordinary or even unanimous majorities are to be preferred. Compare the Articles which called for at least a majority of nine of the thirteen states in all important cases. From this view of federalism it further followed that a league had no business with the individual citizens of the member states, the governing of them remaining the business of the states. In its limited activities, the central body was to deal only with *its* "citizens," i.e., the sovereign states.

According to the Framers, then, a federal system was federal in three main ways. First, the member states were equals in the making of the central decisions. Second, these central agreements were to be carried out by the member states themselves. Third, the confederal body was not to deal with the vast bulk of political matters; governing, for all practical purposes, remained with the member states. Given this view of the meaning of federalism, we can readily see why the Framers could not possibly regard the new Constitution as merely a federal system, but rather regarded it as a "composition" of both federal and national elements.

## II

The Federal Convention began its work by considering the detailed plan carefully prepared in advance and presented to it by the Virginia delegation. The Virginia Plan proposed the creation of a powerful government which it throughout described by the shocking term *national*. It clearly went far beyond the common understanding that the Convention was only to propose amendments to the existing Confederacy. The great issue so abruptly placed before the Convention was made perfectly explicit when Governor Randolph, at the suggestion of Gouverneur Morris, proposed a substitution for the initial clause of the Virginia Plan. The original formulation was: "Resolved that the articles of Confederation ought to be so corrected and enlarged, as to accomplish the objects proposed by their institution; namely, common defense, security of liberty and general welfare."[11] The substitute formulation left no possible doubt about how far the Virginia Plan went. Resolved "that a Union of the States merely federal will not accomplish the objects proposed by the articles of Confederation, namely common defense, security of

[11] *Ibid.,* p. 116.

liberty, and general welfare"; and resolved further "that a *national* Government ought to be established consisting of a *supreme* Legislative, Executive and Judiciary."[12]

Randolph said, in short: by the Articles we meant to insure our defense, liberty and general welfare; they failed; no system of the merely federal kind will secure these things for us; we must create a supreme, that is, national government.

Discussion centered on the resolution proposing a national and supreme government. Oddly enough, the resolution was almost immediately adopted, six states to one. At this moment the Convention was pointed to a simply national government, and not the "composition" which finally resulted. But the matter was not to be so easily settled, not least because several small state delegations, which happened to be federally minded, subsequently arrived. Despite the favorable vote on the Randolph resolution, the Convention had not yet truly made up their mind. Too many delegates remained convinced federalists. They would have to be persuaded to change their minds or the final plan would have to be compromised so as to accommodate the wishes of those who would not go so far as a straightforwardly national plan. Therefore, as specific portions of the Virginia Plan were discussed in the ensuing weeks, the fundamental issue—a federal versus a national plan—came up again and again.

The most important feature of the discussions is the following. The Convention had originally squared off on the issue of federalism *versus* nationalism, the true federalists regarding nationalism as fatal to liberty, the nationalists regarding confederalism as "imbecilically" incompetent. Compromise would have been impossible across the gulf of two such opposed views. One or the other of the two original views had to be modified so that the distance between the two could be bridged by compromise. And that is precisely what happened. After three weeks of discussion, the issue had subtly changed. The opponents of a purely national government found themselves unable to defend the pure federal principle. The simple nationalists remained such in principle, while the pure federalists implicitly found themselves forced to acknowledge the inadequacy of the federal

[12] *Ibid.*, p. 120.

principle. Now the question was between those still advocating a purely national plan and those who, having abandoned a purely federal scheme, were determined only to work some federal features into the final outcome. Thus the famous compromise, the "composition" which finally resulted, was a compromise between the simple nationalists and half-hearted federalists, i.e., federalists who were themselves moving toward the national principle. Only because of this underlying victory of the simple nationalists was the issue finally made capable of compromise.

This does not mean that the pure federalists yielded easily or completely. The ideas which led them to their federalist position had a powerful hold over their minds. A fundamental theoretical issue, as we shall see, had to be raised before they could be made substantially to retreat from their federalist position. And, even then, important concessions had finally to be made to the unconvinced and only partially convinced. Moreover, the ideas supporting that federalist position have long retained their vitality in American politics; and the federal elements which finally found their way into the Constitution have always supplied historical and legal support to recurring expressions of the traditional federalist view. It is necessary to acknowledge the survival of this view and the grounds for its survival. But it is impossible to understand the work of the Convention without seeing that the view survived only after having first been shaken to its very root, and hence that it survived only in a permanently weakened condition.

How this happened is perfectly revealed in a notable exchange between Madison, straightforwardly for the national plan at that point, and Sherman of Connecticut, one of the intelligent defenders of the federal principle.

> The objects of Union [Sherman] thought were *few*. 1. defence against foreign danger. 2. against internal disputes & a resort to force. 3. Treaties with foreign nations. 4. regulating foreign commerce, & drawing revenue from it. These & perhaps a few lesser objects *alone rendered a confederation of the States necessary.* All other matters civil & criminal would be much better in the hands of the States. *The people are more happy in small than in large States.*[13]

[13] *Ibid.*, pp. 160–61. Italics supplied.

Whereas Madison

> differed from the member from Connecticut in thinking
> the objects mentioned to be all the principal ones that re-
> quired a National Government. Those were certainly im-
> portant and necessary objects; but he combined with them
> the necessity of providing more effectually for the security
> of private rights, and the steady dispensation of Justice. In-
> terferences with these were evils which had more perhaps
> than anything else, produced this convention. Was it to be
> supposed that republican liberty could long exist under the
> abuses of it practised in some of the States.[14]

Madison was skillfully pressing a sensitive nerve. Not only were
the delegates concerned with the inadequacy of the Confederacy for
"general" purposes, but nearly all were also unhappy with the way
things had been going in the states themselves since the Revolution.
Above all, the delegates agreed in fearing the tendency in many of
the states to agrarian and debtors' measures that seemed to threaten
the security of property. The Shays' Rebellion, for example, had
terrified many of the delegates. Sherman had himself, after the
passage quoted above, adverted to this dangerous tendency, and
had, moreover, admitted that "too small" states were by virtue of
their smallness peculiarly "subject to faction." Madison seized upon
this.

> The gentleman had admitted that in a very small State,
> faction & oppression would prevail. It was to be inferred
> then that wherever these prevailed the State was too small.
> Had they not prevailed in the largest as well as the smallest
> tho' less than in the smallest; and were we not thence ad-
> monished to enlarge the sphere as far as the nature of the
> Government would admit. This was the only defence
> against the inconveniencies of democracy consistent with
> the democratic form of Government.[15]

Sherman, the defender of the federal principle, considered the
ends of union to be few. Madison, the defender of the national
principle, considered the ends of union to be many. Sherman would
leave the most important matters of government to the individual

[14] *Ibid.*, pp. 161–62.
[15] *Ibid.*, p. 162.

states. Madison would place the most important matters—e.g., "security of private rights, and the steady dispensation of justice"— under a national government. Sherman believed that the people would be happiest when governed by their individual states, these being the natural dwelling place of republicanism. Madison believed that republican liberty would perish under the states and that therefore the people would be happiest when under a national government; only such a government made possible the very large republic which in turn supplied the democratic remedy for the inconveniences of democracy.

Madison, then, argued with Sherman and the other defenders of the federal principle in two ways. First, he appealed to the delegates to acknowledge that they really wanted very much more from union than Sherman admitted. We will see how the Convention's decisive action turned on just this issue. The fact that nearly all the delegates, themselves included, wanted a very great deal from union became *the* stumbling block to the defenders of a federal plan. As we shall see, the explicit endorsement of a national plan dramatically followed the most powerful showing of how much was wanted from union and how little could be supplied by the federal principle. But it would not have sufficed merely to demonstrate the incompatibility of federalism and a union from which much was desired. The delegates could still have done what any man can do who has two equal and contradictory desires. They could have abandoned their preference for the federal principle in favor of firm union, as Madison wished, or they could have abandoned a firm union in favor of the federal principle, as Madison emphatically did not wish. Madison therefore had also to give the delegates a reason to choose only one of the two incompatible alternatives, namely, a firm union under a national government. This meant persuading the delegates to renounce their attachment to federalism. And that is precisely what Madison attempted. He sought to undermine that attachment by supplying a new solution to the problem for which federalism had been the traditional answer.

The best men, like Sherman, who defended the federal principle at the Convention, and those, like R. H. Lee, who subsequently opposed adoption of the Constitution, did not defend federalism for its own sake. Who could? They defended the federal principle against the plan of a national or primarily national government because they thought they were thereby defending a precious thing, namely, republican liberty. They saw a connection between republicanism and federalism. They regarded federalism as the sole way in which some of the advantages of great size could be obtained by those who wanted to enjoy the blessings of republicanism. This view rested on two considerations. First, it argued that only small countries can possess republican government. Second, it argued that, when such small republics seek the advantages of greater size, they can preserve their republicanism by uniting only in a federal way. This was the view Madison had to undermine. The small-republic idea is now half-forgotten and needs some restoration before its hold upon the true federalists of the founding generation can be appreciated.

The true federalists decisively rested their case on the proposition that only the state governments, and not some huge national government, could be made or kept truly free and republican. In this they were following the very old belief, popularized anew in the way men understood Montesquieu, that only small countries could enjoy republican government. The reasoning that supported the belief ran something as follows. Large countries necessarily turn to despotic rule. For one thing, large countries need despotic rule; political authority breaks down if the central government does not govern more forcefully than the republican form admits. Further, large countries, usually wealthy and populous, are warlike by nature or are made warlike by envious neighbors; such belligerency nurtures despotic rule. Moreover, not even the best intentions suffice to preserve the republicanism of a large country. To preserve their rule, the people must be patriotic, vigilant, and informed. This requires that the people give loving attention to public things, and that the affairs of the country be on a scale commensurate with the people's understanding. But in large countries the people, baffled and rendered apathetic by the complexity of public affairs, at last become absorbed in their own pursuits. Finally, even were the citizens of a large republic able to remain alert, they must allow a few men actually to conduct the public business. Far removed from the localities and possessed of the instruments of coercion, the necessarily trusted representatives would inevitably subvert the republican rule to their own passions and interests. Such was the traditional and strongly held view of the necessity that republics be small.

From the small-republic argument, it followed that nothing could be done in the way of union which would subvert the integrity and primacy of the uniting states. *They* must remain the governments of the people. Whatever brought the people directly under the union and made it the government of the people, to that extent undermined *the* precondition of republicanism. *Hence federalism:* the way of combining for limited purposes into a league which preserves the integrity and primacy of the small republics which compose the league.

It is clear, then, that Madison had to persuade the delegates, as it were, that they could have their cake and eat it, too. That is, they could have the firm union that would supply the blessings they wanted, *without* sacrificing the republicanism for which they had hitherto thought federalism was indispensable. Federalism was indispensable only so long as men held to the small-republic theory. And that is the theory Madison tried to demolish. Nothing is more important to an understanding of both the theoretical and practical issues in the founding of the American Republic than a full appreciation of Madison's stand on behalf of the very large republic.

Montesquieu's famous explicit statement conveys the gist of the true federalists' belief. He said that small republics, by virtue of the federal form, could combine "the internal advantages of a republican, together with the external force of a monarchical, government."[16] What does this mean? The necessity that republican countries be small had an unfortunate disadvantage: small republics were often defeated in wars by large monarchies. This was the thing which, as Sherman put it, "rendered a confederation . . . necessary." By federating, small republics can make themselves large enough to be strong against external enemies. Their massive reason for federating is war. Federation preserves their physical existence. But their *republicanism*, in this view, owes nothing to the union; republicanism results from the reservation of the governing of people to the small republics which compose the confederacy.

Madison turned the small-republic argument upside down. On

[16] *The Spirit of Laws,* trans. Thomas Nugent; rev. J. V. Prichard (London: George Bell and Sons, 1878), I, 136.

the contrary, he argued, *smallness* was fatal to republicanism. The small republics of antiquity were wretched nurseries of internal warfare, and the Convention itself had been "produced" by the fear for liberty in the "small" American states. "Was it to be supposed that republican liberty could long exist under the abuses of it practised in some of the States. . . . Were we not then admonished to enlarge the sphere as far as the nature of the Government would admit." Smallness is fatal to republican liberty. Only a country as large as the whole thirteen states and more could provide a safe dwelling-place for republican liberty. Republicanism not only permits but requires taking away from the states responsibility for "the security of private rights, and the steady dispensation of Justice," else rights and justice will perish under the state governments.

This was the great and novel idea which came from the Convention: a large, powerful republic with a competent national government regulated under a wise Constitution.

## III

It is startling to see at the Convention how far some of the most famous Founders dared to go in a simply national direction. And it is startling to discover how close they came to succeeding completely. The issue came to a head with the introduction and discussion of the New Jersey Plan. Mr. Patterson of New Jersey asked the Convention's leave to prepare, in opposition to the Virginia Plan, a "purely federal" plan. But by now the arguments of Madison and others had had their effect. Even this desperate effort of several small states and other truly federally minded delegates to whittle down the emerging Constitution moved far beyond the Articles in the ends and powers it proposed for the Union. In addition to preserving all the functions and powers of the existing Confederacy, the New Jersey Plan proposed the creation of a federal executive and judiciary, gave the Congress authority over foreign and interstate trade, supplied the Union with a taxing power and thus a revenue source independent of the states, made all confederal laws and treaties "the supreme law of the respective states," and empowered the federal executive to use the armed force of the Confederacy to compel the compliance of recalcitrant states. All this went very far indeed, and the last provision for military coercion was an amazing grant of power. It proved, however, the Achilles heel of the Patterson Plan.

Far from being appeased by Patterson's concessions, the most nationally minded delegates descended upon the New Jersey Plan. The long discussion of fundamentals now neared its climax. The advocates of the Virginia Plan exulted that the pure federalists now admitted, in the New Jersey Plan, how broad the governing powers must be to achieve the blessings of union, and that legislative, executive, and judicial organs of government were needed for their application. But they pointed out that the attempt to achieve these things *by purely federal means* led to Patterson's ludicrous reliance upon military coercion, upon civil war as the means to secure the blessings of union.

In a masterful speech, Madison concluded the attack on the New Jersey Plan. The heart of the speech is a full and persuasive statement of *all* the things that *all* the delegates knew they wanted from union. Of course, he argued, we all want what Sherman had earlier acknowledged: defense against foreign enemies, prevention of armed conflict among the member states, treaties with foreign nations. But even the Articles of Confederation had gone beyond these familiar aims of confederation. Under the Articles, we had all wanted *America* to deal with that peculiar problem of foreign relations, the Indians; the vast western lands to be controlled by and used on behalf of the whole country; protection against piracy on the seas; the states to be made to comply with the obligations of treaties; with an eye to a unified commerce, citizens from all states to enjoy equal protection under any state's laws, and the legal proceedings of any one state to be given full faith and credit in all the states; an end to restrictions on commerce among the states; and prevention of the growth of dominant states that would oppress the others.

All this was wanted by all, even under the "weak" Articles of Confederation. The point that Madison does not make explicitly should be made in passing: the Articles did not fail because of their weakness as such, but rather because Americans sought so much under them. The Confederacy under the Articles was not a weak league. On the contrary, it was a very good league as leagues go. Measured against other confederacies and by standards appropriate to confederacies, the Confederacy comes off very well. But that was not how the delegates were measuring it. They were measuring it by standards appropriate to nations, because they wanted from the central body what only a national government could supply. *The Federalist,* for example, bludgeons the opponents of the Constitution with this argument. And Madison, in this speech of June 19, effectively addressed it to the delegates.

Madison did not stop with a demonstration of how many national things had already been sought under the Articles. Much more was now wanted. The delegates wanted, and they knew they wanted, central economic controls over the states, that is, over matters hitherto regarded as inviolably belonging to the member states: for instance, controls over "the emissions of paper money & other kindred measures."[17] The delegates wanted, he argued, the central body to guarantee "the *internal* tranquility of the States themselves."[18] The delegates wanted the *Union* to "secure a good *internal* legislation & administration to the particular States."[19]

> In developing the evils which vitiate the political system of the U.S. it is proper to take into view those which prevail *within the States individually* as well as those which affect them collectively: Since the former indirectly affect the whole; and there is great reason to believe that the pressure of them had a full share in the motives which produced the present Convention. Under this head he enumerated and animadverted on 1. the multiplicity of the laws passed by the several States. 2. the mutability of their laws. 3. the injustice of them. 4. the impotence of them: observing that Mr. Patterson's plan contained no remedy for this dreadful class of evils, and could not therefore be received as an adequate provision for the exigencies of the Community.[20]

The delegates, Madison argued, knew that the creation of a union adequate to the achievement of all these things in their fullness was the real task of the Convention. Here was where all were agreed. Now the delegates must surely see that no federal system could accomplish the desired ends. If, as under the Articles, coercion

[17] *Documents ...*, p. 230.
[18] *Idem.* Italics supplied.
[19] *Idem.* Italics supplied.
[20] *Ibid.*, pp. 230–31. Italics supplied.

was denied, the ends would go by default; it would be as if there were no union. If, as proposed by New Jersey, military coercion were to be employed, the ends would be sought by means subversive of all decency and which would "bring confusion and ruin upon the whole."[21]

Apparently the very instant Madison ceased speaking, matters were put to the vote. The Convention decided, seven states to three, against the "purely federal" Patterson plan, thereby making Randolph's plan to introduce a "national government" the basic document before the Convention. Again the matter seemed to have been settled in favor of a simply national plan, but again more had to happen. The very next day, Ellsworth of Connecticut, one of the federal delegates, sought to lessen somewhat the force of the previous day's vote reinstating the Randolph plan. He proposed to alter the wording of the Randolph resolve "that a *national* government ought to be established consisting of a Supreme Legislative, Executive & Judiciary."[22]

> [He moved] to alter it so as to run "that the Government of the United States ought to consist of a supreme legislative, Executive and Judiciary." This alteration he said would drop the word *national,* and retain the proper title "the United States."[23]

So far had this intelligent man been driven.[24] He agreed to a *government*. He agreed to its *supremacy*. And because it was to be the supreme government he agreed to giving it its "proper title." He asked only that "the word *national*" be dropped. Randolph promptly agreed to "the change of expression," although he also entered a demurrer against any far-reaching implications of the change. Understandably the proponents of the Virginia Plan made no further issue of the matter, and Ellsworth's proposal was adopted without dissent. Never again was there a reversion to a primarily

[21] *Ibid.,* p. 229.
[22] *Ibid.,* p. 234. Italics supplied.
[23] *Ibid.,* p. 240.
[24] Ellsworth and Sherman later wrote essays in support of the Constitution under the pseudonyms "Centinel" and "Landholder." These essays reveal plainly the extent to which Madison had convinced them of the possibility of a large republic.

federal plan. But now began the Convention's detailed work, now began the putting together of the Constitution. The outcome was that "composition" of federal and national elements of which *The Federalist* speaks.

The foregoing does not tell us what that "composition" was as it came from the Framers' hands, let alone what it has come to be.[25] Very much more is required for the understanding of the federal issue in the Constitution. For one thing, the Framers were not themselves unanimous regarding the actual character of the document they framed. Further, the Constitution was ratified on the basis of many understandings. And there have been since nearly two centuries of amendment, interpretation, and the sheer working of great events and massive changes in our way of life. All these things must be taken into account in an understanding of what the Constitution was and is. The present essay does not pretend to supply such an understanding, not even of the isolated federal issue.

As the title of the paper indicates, the subject is not what the Constitution means with respect to the federal issue, but what the Framers (and the framing generation) meant by the the term federal when they were considering that issue. Only that is claimed. Other important questions regarding federalism then and now come immediately to mind. And only when we have explored and rightly answered these questions will we understand our obligations, that is, what the Constitution and the Framers demand of us by the authority of law and wisdom. Only this much is further claimed: the other important questions must be considered in the light of what the Framers meant when they considered the federal issue; the right answers depend in good part on the kind of restoration of the Framers' thought that was the intention of this paper.

[25] The author has discussed the nature of the "composition" in "*The Federalist*'s View of Federalism," in *Essays in Federalism* (Claremont, Cal.: Institute for Studies in Federalism, 1962).

Russell Kirk

•

# THE PROSPECTS FOR TERRITORIAL DEMOCRACY IN AMERICA

A century ago, Orestes Brownson wrote that the United States of America form a republic in which territorial democracy prevails.[1] The general or federal institutions were republican, not democratic, in character: that is, the federal Constitution deliberately erected barriers against direct popular control of the national political apparatus. But in states and localities, the mass of the people enjoyed strong powers and rights—"territorial democracy." This manner of democracy Brownson contrasted with "Jacobin democracy," the infatuation with an abstract, infallible People, and the concentration of "popular" power in an absolute, centralized government.

Only a generation before Brownson wrote, Tocqueville had described and praised the institutions of this territorial democracy, in which he saw a principal safeguard against democratic despotism and enervating centralization. The New England town meeting is the perfect example of territorial democracy at work; but analogous institutions existed from the first in the counties of the southern states; and upon one pattern or another, territorial democracy was established in every new state that joined the Union. At the levels of village, town, and county, direct election of officials and local determination of policies—often important policies—was the American frame of politics from the seventeenth century onward. From drain commissioners to county judges; from village constables to county—and often state—school boards; from rural road-building to highly organized urban police departments—in the concerns of

[1] Orestes Brownson, *The American Republic* (1866).

43

government which most immediately affect the public, territorial democracy was adopted everywhere, and almost without challenge.

One form of territorial democracy has been the state governments, hostile toward centralization of authority in Washington, and generally suspicious of executive authority, whether in Washington or as represented even by the state governors. Elected from comparatively small constituencies, and holding only short legislative sessions, the state senators and representatives generally have been much more closely identified with popular opinion than have the members of Congress. Beyond the Mississippi, indeed, the concept and the reality of territorial democracy formed the states, rather than territorial democracy gradually arising in old political territories; for while the highly arbitrary and abstract boundaries of the western states represent nothing but cartographers' and congressmen's convenience, still the institution and practice of territorial democracy have given to Montana and Arizona and Kansas, say, some distinct and peculiar character as political territories, by fixing loyalties and forming an enduring structure of political administration.[2]

Among states politically stable, only in Switzerland has territorial democracy been carried further than in the United States. In America, centralization on principle has had few avowed champions. Among the leaders of the early republic, only one—Alexander Hamilton—would have preferred a political structure more concentrated than the present Constitution of the United States and the existing state constitutions and local establishments. Although leaders of factions so hostile toward one another as John Adams, Thomas Jefferson, and John Randolph differed greatly upon questions of national and state policy, they shared an attachment to the reality of territorial democracy—that is, local control of by far the greater part of political activity. Here they differed in degree, but not in principle.

[2] As John Randolph declared in Congress in 1828, in the beginning the Western states were not properly political territories in the true sense, and giving inchoate and almost uninhabited regions a voice in the Senate equal to that of ancient and populous political communities, possessed of traditions and property, was political injustice. But since then, the stabilizing and conservative influence of the pattern of territorial democracy has joined with increase of population and wealth to make sensible political territories of what originally were mere parallelograms of prairie and desert and forest.

# The Prospects for Territorial Democracy in America

"Federalism" is not altogether a satisfactory term of politics. In the beginning, the word implied "league," rather than union; and doubtless the majority of Americans who voted to ratify the Federal Constitution thought they were approving merely a more efficient form of the Articles of Confederation; it was sufficiently difficult, indeed, to persuade them to accept the Constitution even upon such an understanding. Yet the structure created at Philadelphia amounted to a new pattern of government, not truly federal in the old sense. As John Adams put it, in his concluding observations of his *Defence of the Constitutions:*

> The former confederation of the United States was formed upon the model and example of all the confederacies, ancient and modern, in which the federal council was only a diplomatic body.... The magnitude of territory, the population, the wealth and commerce, and especially the rapid growth of the United States, have shown such a government to be inadequate to their wants; and the new system, which seems admirably calculated to unite their interests and affections, and bring them to an uniformity of principles and sentiments, is equally well combined to unite their wills and forces as a nation.

Thus the success of the American Republic has altered the usage of the very word "federalism," which no longer is generally taken to mean a simple league of sovereign states. Nowadays the signification of this term is adequately expressed by the third definition offered in *The Century Dictionary* (edition of 1904):

> Pertaining to a union of states in some essential degree constituted by and deriving its power from the people of all, considered as an entirety, and not solely by and from each of the states separately; as a *federal* government, such as the governments of the United States, Switzerland, and some of the Spanish-American republics. A *federal* government is properly one in which the federal authority is independent of any of its component parts within the sphere of the federal action: distinguished from a *confederate* government, in which the states alone are sovereign, and which possesses no inherent power.

Yet this is not all. "Federalism" still implies a voluntary and limited union for certain defined purposes, rather than a central system of government. In his important essay "Federalism and Freedom," Professor Werner Kägi of Zurich distinguishes five characteristics of federalism: (*a*) federalism is an order of "multiplicity in unity"; (*b*) federalism is an order that is based upon the autonomy of the narrower communities; (*c*) federalism is an order in which the smaller circles and communities are granted the maximum possible power to direct their own affairs; (*d*) federalism is an order which makes it possible for minorities to live together in freedom; (*e*) federalism is an order built upwards from the smaller communities, in which the conditions can, to a certain degree, be seen at a glance, and in which relationships have, to a certain degree, remained on a personal footing.[3]

As Dr. Kägi points out, the spirit of federalism sometimes subsists in political systems that do not bear the formal label "federal"— as in Britain, where in practice and by prescription county and town authorities retain great permanent rights and powers, though in theory Parliament is supreme under the Crown. And some orders that still are called "federal" have ceased, in large part, so to operate. In general, one may say that a modern federal order divides power between a general government and territorial governments, with the aim of safeguarding local liberties while securing national interests.

What does this have to do with "territorial democracy"? Well, American democracy, so unanimously and vaguely praised, essentially is territorial or local in character. The general government in Washington is not democratic, but representative and republican. In the phrase of Madison, "A democracy . . . will be confined to a small spot. A republic may be extended over a large region." So it is that Brownson wrote of *The American Republic*, not the American democracy; and so it is that Tocqueville, describing American democratic institutions, places such emphasis upon state and local government. The most celebrated champions of democracy, indeed, have not expected democracy ever to be expressed in a national government. "God alone can rule the *world*," says Rousseau, "and to govern great nations requires superhuman qualities." The ad-

[3] Werner Kägi, "Federalism and Freedom," in Hunold (ed.), *Freedom and Serfdom, an Anthology of Western Thought* (Dordrecht: D. Reindel Publishing Company, 1961).

vocates of centralization have not been practical democrats, but rather administrators (whether or not levelling in their social proclivities) like Turgot, an intendant of the Old Regime, who wrote to Dr. Price that in America the people should collect "all authority into one centre, the nation." To this, John Adams replied:

> It is easily understood how all authority may be collected into "one centre" in a despot or monarch; but how it may be done when the centre is to be the nation, is much more difficult to comprehend. . . . If, after the pains of "collecting all authority into one centre," that centre is to be the nation, we shall remain exactly where we began, and no collection of authority at all will be made. The nation will be the authority, and the authority the nation. The centre will be the circle, and the circle the centre. When a number of men, women, and children, are simply congregated together, there is no political authority among them; nor any natural authority, but that of parents over their children.

To resort to a word cherished by Ambrose Bierce, truly central government and true democracy are incompossible. The American "federal" system was adopted to perpetuate and protect and improve the institutions of territorial democracy which already existed in America—even though the phrase "territorial democracy" was not then employed. If the federal character of American government decays badly, then American democracy also must decline terribly, until nothing remains of it but a name; and the new "democrats" may be economic and social levellers, indeed, but they will give popular government short shrift. As Kägi puts it, *"A political entity remains free and human only for as long as it preserves, even in the face of radically altered circumstances, at least something of its federal structure. For my own country, Switzerland, this is a conditio sine qua non;* but it is a principle which applies equally to each and every political entity." Or, as Dr. Felix Morley applies this principle to the United States:

> Our organic law seeks to harmonize all government action with the talent of a truly free people for self-government. They remain free only as long as they maintain this spiritual aspiration. Without faith, the Constitution fails. Whether or not our Federal Republic will be maintained is therefore

at bottom a moral issue. It depends as much on the churches and the synagogues as on the legislators and the law courts. The growth of Big Government goes hand in hand with the loss of Big Conviction.[4]

Federalism, *modern* federalism, in fine, is a device to reconcile self-government—territorial democracy—with the great exigencies of the nation-state. If the federal character of government vanishes, it still may be possible to maintain national strength—though even here, among a people long accustomed to self-government, there are grave difficulties. But in such an eventuality, it will not be possible to retain the institutions of orderly and genuine democracy. Many of the ardent advocates of centralization being at the same time ardent democrats, they ought to confront this conundrum with something better than cries of "The people, yes!"

Though not truly "federal" in the older sense of that word, the American constitutional system has succeeded, most of the time, in dividing power justly between the general government and the state governments, and in providing for national necessities. "When it is not necessary to change," said Falkland, "it is necessary not to change." So a heavy burden of proof rests upon the advocates of centralization in America: by imprudent alteration, we would run severe risk of an enduring constriction of freedom and order. Tocqueville pointed out the ingenuity and real benefits of the American federal device:

> The human understanding more easily invents new things than new words, and we are hence constrained to employ many improper and inadequate expressions. When several nations form a permanent league and establish a supreme authority, which, although it cannot act upon private individuals like a national government, still acts upon each of the confederate states in a body, this government, which is so essentially different from all others, is called Federal. Another form of society is afterwards discovered in which several states are fused into one with regard to certain com-

---

[4] Felix Morley, *Freedom and Federalism* (Chicago: Henry Regnery Company, 1959), p. 240.

mon interests, although they remain distinct, or only confederate, with regard to all other concerns. In this case the central power acts directly upon the governed, whom it rules and judges in the same manner as a national government, but in a more limited circle. Evidently this is no longer a federal government, but an incomplete national government, which is neither exactly national nor exactly federal; but the new word which ought to express this novel thing does not yet exist.

Ignorance of this new species of confederation has been the cause that has brought all unions to civil war, to servitude, or to inertness; and the states which formed these leagues have been either too dull to discern, or too pusillanimous to apply, this great remedy. The first American Confederation perished by the same defects.[5]

Though this "federal" system that really is an "incomplete national government" has worked remarkably well, fulfilling the five characteristics of real federalism that Professor Kägi distinguishes, there exist Americans who would like to convert it into a complete national government.

Even today, few practical politicians openly advocate political centralization and the removal of power from the hands of the citizenry. The Republican leadership advocates a "new federalism," to be made possible through the return of a portion of federal income-tax revenues to the states; the Democrats have modified somewhat their centralizing tendencies conspicuous in 1960, and such Democrats as Mr. Richard Goodwin declare that centralization is a curse to our age. For the notion of "plebiscitary" or Jacobin democracy, far from obtaining public sanction, remains confined to small circles of governmental administrators, professors, trade-union officers, and lobbyists for certain special-interest groups.

For all that, territorial democracy is insecure in these United States, and the process of its weakening has been observable for a century. The Civil War was a victory for national unity; but also, as Brownson saw—though he adhered to the northern cause—it was a blow against territorial democracy. The Reconstruction Amendments to the Constitution further confused and obscured the dis-

[5] Alexis de Tocqueville, *Democracy in America*, ed. Phillips Bradley (New York: Alfred A. Knopf, 1945), Vol. I, pp. 158–59.

tinction between a unitary, centralized system and the voluntary association of territorial democracies into states and a republic. Ever since the Civil War, with only occasional exceptions, the tendency of the federal courts has been to exalt central governmental powei above state and local claims; in the past decade, this drift has become almost an ideological predilection in the Supreme Court. And the concentration of military and economic power in Washington that has resulted from the Second World War and the contest with the Soviets, together with the vast increase in the proportion of federal taxation, more and more have given territorial democracy an archaic appearance.

In an age of increasing economic concentration, mobility of population, and stern military necessity, to some degree it is inevitable that the political patterns of an era more peaceful and less urban undergo marked change. Speedways require state traffic patrolmen; the sprawl of the suburbs requires prudent reorganization of old local political boundaries; the sudden rise of population in Tennessee or New Mexico because of governmental projects requires, for instance, federal subsidies in aid of local schools directly affected.

For the man who takes long views, then, our pressing necessity seems to be the reconciliation of the principal aspects of territorial democracy with such reform and consolidation as appear essential. But not enough people pay any attention to this problem; and some strong pressure-groups are quite ready to sweep away territorial democracy altogether, in favor of a centralized system which would surpass even Jacobin democracy in its unitary character and—if justly it could be called democracy at all—perhaps is better described as "plebiscitary democracy."

Why are some persons in positions of influence indifferent to the menace of centralization, or else reluctant to confront the problem? Why do certain American politicians and a good many leaders of American pressure-groups repeat, like incantations, phrases about "the ultimate truth of democracy" and "the fundamental wisdom of the People"—when, at the same time, they advocate legislation that would transfer power from public bodies genuinely democratic to an executive authority almost unrestrained? Why, for instance, do certain gentlemen who repeatedly and vociferously affirm their unqualified faith in "the democratic way of life" at the same time recommend that more and more categories of cases be transferred from regular courts of law to the jurisdiction of recently-created administrative tribunals, not governed by the "democratic process?"

Well, the causes of this inconsistency are several. Logically, one can maintain such a position only if one subscribes to Turgot's notion that "the nation shall be the centre, and the centre the nation": that is, to the doctrine, an example of what Burke called "metaphysical madness," that somehow the People may act as a whole, through a central government, in an abstract, infallible Democracy.

But few of the centralizers go so far. Most of them do not recommend, or see as immediately possible, the culmination of this movement in a thoroughgoing centralization of power. They are willing to allow the states and even local units of government to remain as junior partners in the system, supposing these do not presume to assert any claims to distinct powers or rights. Yet the centralizers' general assumption is that authorities in Washington should make the important decisions, and that the state and local governments should obey promptly. This may be called partnership; but in reality it would be a dissolution of the Constitutional partnership, and a gradual emerging of a new relationship: master and servants. And the new master would be far more difficult to restrain, if unjust or in error, than the present state and local authorities.

Not logic, then, but a humanitarianism that thrusts aside political theory, and sometimes the immediate advantages of a particular group, are the sources of the centralizing movement. Yet in the long run there may result from these impulses certain political consequences which the humanitarian and the well-intentioned member of a pressure-group never foresaw. It is infinitely difficult to push the federal government back out of a field into which it has been drawn.

Piecemeal, then, rather than by any grand design, centralization of political authority proceeds in this country. No man can predict precisely when the nation may cross the line of demarcation that distinguishes a federal system from a unitary structure. "Government is force," President Washington said. Having transferred gradually all real power from state and local authorities to "federal" authorities, the humanitarian or special-interest advocates of increased activities by the general government may find that, almost in a fit of absence of mind, they have created a unitary power-structure which can be resisted by no one. Only power restrains power; and impotent state and local "governments" that have been deprived, over the years, of effective decision-making must end unable to hold in check the force of the total state.

These problems produced within the Nixon administration, early in 1970, a debate among members of the White House staff concerning the character of Mr. Nixon's intended "New Federalism." Two youngish gentlemen of opposing views circulated privately their mimeographed broadsides, using pseudonyms in eighteenth-century fashion. "New Publius" (really Mr. William Safire) handed round a little tract entitled "The New Federalism"; "Cato" (actually Mr. Tom Huston) replied with a counterblast, "Federalism, Old and New; or, the Pretensions of New Publius Exposed." This exchange suggests the bigness of the issue with which we deal here.

The New Publius seeks to lead the Nixon administration toward a kind of decentralized centralization: that is, the national government would determine large policies, but the states would carry them out. The resurrected Cato sets his face against this concept—or against portions of it—on the ground that it resembles the "General Will" of Rousseau.

Although William Safire is no thoroughgoing centralizer, his argument about "national conscience" does represent the attitude of those humanitarians who have come to look to Washington for redemption. Publius would have national policies implement a national conscience: state governments would carry out those dictates of collective conscience. National morality is determined not by governmental policy, Publius says, or by churches, or by the leaders of society. "What is moral is what most people who think about morality at all think is moral at a given time," he writes.

Yet any conscience requires tutoring, one may be permitted to remark; what we call "conscience" is merely an impulse to do good and to eschew evil; it is not directly inspired by divine omniscience. Conscience must be founded upon moral principles. From what source would Publius draw a national moral judgment? His sentences are disquieting.

## The Prospects for Territorial Democracy in America

One thinks, for instance, of the New England Puritans, political moralizers, whose attempt to establish a moralistic commonwealth did not long endure. But at least the Puritans had Christian doctrine as bedrock—not merely what "people who think about morality at all think is moral at a given time." Such a Publius might deliver the nation into the hands of a set of secular Pharisees, convinced of their own perfect rectitude, and confident in their ability to enforce their private moral judgments upon the whole people. Did Publius ever reflect upon the Volstead Act and the public reaction against that piece of legislated morality?

"In approaching the question of equity as it applies to the relationship between the individual and government," Cato replies to New Publius, "it must be remembered that the value we seek is justice, not morality. Government is not ordained to dispense morality; it is established to effect justice. And justice, as we understand it, encompasses both the principle by which each man is protected in the things which are his own and the procedures through which that principle is made operative."

A cardinal error in diplomacy, Sir Herbert Butterfield has written more than once, is the arrogance of "righteousness"—that is, to assume that the policies of one's own country are godly and goodly, and that any opposing power must be consummately evil. This is quite as true, I interject here, in the domestic arrangements of great states. To establish a "national conscience" with the power of the general government behind it would be to cast into the outer darkness all those citizens—perhaps a majority—who do not happen to fall in with the moral judgments of the moment made by a Washington Elect. The imposition of an abstract "national conscience" would be grossly unjust; and Cato is right, surely, in declaring that the political order is meant to sustain justice, not to ordain morals.

"There is no such thing as public morality," Cato continues. "There is only a composite of private morality. If government were to define the moral purpose of our society and the moral values of our people, it would also have to enforce adherence to, and prohibit deviations from, that purpose and those values. Under such circumstances, it would no longer be a limited government, but rather a total government that ruled every significant aspect of the individual's life."

It may seem that I have digressed too far here. Yet I have touched upon this contest between New Publius and Cato both because it illustrates the point that federalism and centralization are not merely matters of administrative convenience, but necessarily are bound up with large theoretical and ethical considerations; and because it reveals somewhat the gulf of sentiment which separates the reforming centralizer from the adherent to territorial democracy. On humanitarian impulses, the theoretical centralizer may cry up a new "moral" denomination, in which virtuous men endowed with power will save the people from their sins and errors.

The friend to territorial democracy replies that the idealistic centralizer would be unable to recruit that ethical elect in politics of which he dreams. Does he look for them in the dormitory-town of Washington, so rootless, so corrupt? Or does he expect to create a kind of sanhedrin of university professors, ideologues self-righteous and deficient in practical arts of governance? Would not this centralized elite be composed, rather, of those dull and narrow administrators foreseen by T. S. Eliot in his reply to Karl Mannheim?[6] Or conceivably made up of those rootless and morally barren political people described by Orwell in *1984*?

Moreover, the advocate of territorial democracy argues, the centralizer-on-principle soon finds it necessary to form an alliance with the centralizer for special advantage—with the lobbyists of powerful interests, with the grand contact-men who make fortunes out of the manipulation of federal funds, with many a Bobby Baker and a Billy Sol Estes. So there comes to pass—to quote Randolph of Roanoke, the most relentless adversary of centralization—"the coalition of Blifil and Black George, the Puritan and the blackleg." There exists no evidence to suggest that a centralized political system is more "moral" than a structure of diversity; but one might collect a good deal of evidence to suggest that the centralized system—because more vast, less flexible, and more difficult to restrain or amend—offers less of justice, in the classical definition of that word.

Suppose, nevertheless, that we shrug off these theoretical questions, and settle the debate about centralization and federalism on

---

[6] T. S. Eliot, "The Class and the Elite," in *Notes Towards the Definition of Culture* (London: Faber and Faber, 1948), pp. 35–49.

grounds empirical and pragmatic. Would thoroughgoing centralization indeed bring about greater strength and beneficent reform, practically? Let us consider two very different aspects of centralization: national defense and public instruction.

Even in the realm of national defense, where the Washington authorities have prescriptive precedence, a thoroughgoing centralization might defeat the intentions of its advocates. We are told, for instance, that effective preparation for national security cannot be attained under our present constitutional structure. Yet I am unaware of any hostility by state or local governments to measures of defense and survival. If the federal government sets out a coherent plan for building shelters, creating stockpiles, relocating some industries, redesigning urban centers, and the like, it seems certain we can count upon state and local co-operation. Surely it is unnecessary to go further than offering federal grants-in-aid. What we have lacked in this field is not state and local good will, but rather any general design from Washington. If there has been negligence, the fault has lain with the very general government upon which the centralizers would load fresh responsibilities.

Something more: today one of the principal perils from atomic attack is that missiles might destroy the centers of command, so rendering resistance leaderless throughout a country. Just that would happen in centralized France, presumably, if Paris were to be destroyed, while federal Australia or Canada would be less injured. Sound preparation for such a blow requires that authority be widely diffused throughout a nation, and that state and local leaders be accustomed to decision-making, able to maintain the fabric of order even if the national capital is smashed. By concentrating powers of decision in the federal apparatus—necessarily, for the most part, in Washington—the centralizers' system seems calculated to increase, rather than diminish, risk of disruption by a single military attack. Of all times in our history, the present is the era when we need healthy and self-reliant state and local governments.

It may be argued that decentralization can be achieved through delegation of powers to agencies of the federal government in various regions and cities, rather than through the existing complex of territorial democracy. This is true enough, in the sense that instructions could be left with the commanding officer of a rocket-launching installation in Colorado, say, to go on firing at the adversary even if Washington should cease to exist. But in the long-run and larger sense, resistance to the enemy and the recovery of order and vigor would have to come from persons deriving their influence from local trust and consent, through established political institutions with deep roots: not to the postmaster or nearest internal-revenue agent, but to the governor or mayor or township supervisor, people would turn in the hour of disaster. And if the old state and local authorities had been so deprived of real exercise of power, and so accustomed to wait upon word from Washington, as to cease to be genuine leaders of community—why, even an American counterpart of Gambetta would succeed no better than did Gambetta in 1871, or Pétain in 1940.

Who seeks guidance in time of crisis from the clerk of the federal district court, the handiest representative of the Department of Agriculture, or the state administrator of the National Defense Education Act? A nation cannot be led by district offices of the Federal Bureau of Investigation, nor even by generals operating upon contingent orders from a source subsequently effaced. Obedience and sacrifice, in such circumstances, may be obtained only by men generally recognized as the expression of state and local popular will: the responsible politician, if you will, not the civil servant or the commander of troops. What, then, if the springs of territorial democracy have been exhausted?

But this argument about national defense deals only with an unknowable future. The case for territorial democracy may be better put by examining the arguments advanced for centralizing proposals that do not immediately involve national survival.

So we take up centralization in public instruction. In 1965, for the first time the federal government appropriated huge general subsidies for public schools. Initially, this pleased organizations that had long lobbied for "federal aid." Yet the consequences already dishearten some early enthusiasts.

Why did the National Education Association and its affiliates, for instance, labor so zealously for federal subsidies to the schools? It is improbable that the typical superintendent of schools desires centralized, authoritarian government, or even plebiscitary democracy—if ever he has heard of the latter. So far as the average superintendent reflects upon general political questions, probably he does not desire to be supervised from Washington, nor intend that the central government should subsidize local police forces, say, on a scale equal to that of aid for the public schools. He is a centralizer only so far as the immediate interests of his own groups are involved.

But the educationists of the public schools thought, in 1965, that it would be easier to obtain ample funds for the schools through congressional appropriation than through state and local political agencies. Everybody's money is nobody's money, and the economies which citizens demand in a village or city or even a state may be forgotten when the funds come from the seemingly inexhaustible coffers of Washington. Beyond this, the transfer of school financing to a central bureaucracy would mean the effectual transfer of school control to the same hands—which hands the officers of the NEA believed, would be the hands of their own members of their allies, what with the interlocking directorate of the NEA and the federal Office of Education. At present, a strong movement for the reform and restoration of schooling gains strength in America. So long as state and local control prevails, such citizen-sponsored reforms are difficult for the educationist establishment to resist. But once effective control of policy should pass from local school boards to a central bureaucracy, the friends of the present educational establishment would have little to dread from "laymen" in education—or so they thought.

With such special-interest groups as the NEA have been leagued a number of intellectuals who desire a grandiose centralization of authority, of which schooling would be only a part. An example of this type of mind is Dr. Henry S. Kariel, who holds that "to put it bluntly, government must be centralized to carry out the tasks of public regulation. Virtually all our problems today are national problems, and they must be dealt with nationally." The schools are part of this consolidation, he continues: "Initially, this will require joining educational government and general government at the local level. But as we recognize that no relation obtains between the mélange of school districts and the demands of our contemporary political life, more becomes essential. We must regulate the framework of the curriculum, the subsidization of students, the salaries of teachers and administrators, and the construction of plants in accordance with national needs and national standards arrived at publicly."[7]

There's candor for you. Usually the centralizers try to sweeten this dose by arguing that, after all, the federal government already has had a hand in education; and besides, we don't want educational chaos, do we? Nearly half the units of government in the United States are school boards. Why have tens of thousands of school boards? Why not have, perhaps, just one? And these school boards have no right to consider themselves distinct sovereignties.

Now of course it is quite true that school districts are not autonomous authorities: like all other divisions of local government, in theory they are agencies of the state governments, and cannot claim to exercise absolute power in their jurisdiction. No one ever held otherwise. Yet the fact remains that in the majority of states, local school boards determine the curriculum, supervise the finances, and appoint the administrators and teachers—that is, they exercise the really important prerogatives of government. This local power tends to produce local interest in schooling, and enables the school system to raise money with less complaint than it could do otherwise; it gives the population a feeling of close representation and of making voluntary grants for the support of public schools. The boards' existence is fully justified.

The fact that we have tens of thousands of school districts in the United States does not mean that we are enduring educational chaos—any more than the existence of tens of thousands of city, county, township, and village governments means that we are enduring political chaos. On the contrary, it means that we still are experiencing territorial democracy, healthy voluntary participation in an important public function. This system is not wasteful, for the emoluments of school-board members are negligible—far less costly than the salaries of civil servants who would replace them under centralization.

Be that as it may, for the past seven years the government at Washington has allocated enormous sums to the public schools— and has steadily extended its practical measures of control over those schools. Laments come from many quarters. Some protest that

[7] Henry S. Kariel, *The Decline of Pluralism* (Stanford: Stanford University Press, 1961), pp. 274–75.

political—nay, ideological—considerations heavily affect policies decreed from Washington; others declare that despite this federal aid—or even because of it—rich school districts grow richer, and poor ones poorer; yet others point out that essential improvements of the troubled system of public instruction are neglected shamefully by Washington, while certain lobbies extract whatever they desire from Congress—the band-uniform lobby, the audio-visual aids lobby, the impacted-districts lobby. And all these complaints have foundation.

One has only to spend a few days in Washington, calling on the gentlemen who allocate federal educational funds, to find that one has to do with the Circumlocution Office. Tremendous programs of research, reform, and innovation are announced from time to time: next to nothing comes of them. We are informed from on high that Washington has commenced a splendid new program of reading-reform, say, adequately financed. Pleased at this prospect, people inquire what method for teaching the art of reading will be employed in the new program. The responsible official replies that this point has not been decided; perhaps it never will be decided, he admits; he confesses, too, that we are failing to teach millions of young people to read satisfactorily; but he hopes to recruit the talents of volunteers—etc., etc. Everything seems amorphous and falsely "spontaneous" as if this were the Academy of Lagado.

How much longer will anyone look to Washington for searching educational reform? We may look, nevertheless, for searching control and direction—the direction, too often, exerted by the unimaginative and complacent. For the man who pays the piper necessarily calls the tune. The chief officer of the National Education Association, on retiring in 1967, lamented to the national convention of his organization that federal educational functionaries were determined to inject political considerations into the federal subsidies. It never could have been otherwise.

The Johnson administration's school-aid measures (adopted, for the most part, as nominally involved with the "war on poverty"), moreover, did next to nothing toward the achieving of equal opportunities in less affluent states and school districts. Because of a "matching funds" provision—unlikely to be repealed—the lion's share of the money has gone to states and districts already relatively well endowed; while really impoverished districts, or many of them, may gain nothing at all, because the intricacy of applying for federal assistance is too much for their overworked administrators.

Finally, the billions of dollars already expended by the federal government have helped little, if at all, to improve the *quality* of American schooling—our real necessity. Our true difficulty here has not been lack of funds, if we compare American expenditures (even of the poorest state) with those of other countries. That true difficulty has been intellectual softness and lack of imagination. These afflictions are not touched by the federal appropriations; and it is quite possible to kill a school, intellectually, with financial largesse.

Many things are not bought with a price. This digression is meant to suggest that in general, as in the instance of federal subsidies to schools, the case for centralization is uneasy; and that possibilities for reform through our present political structure and social institutions have not been exhausted. A uniform national system of public instruction would be deadening to the life of the mind; in the pattern of territorial democracy still lies hope for diversity, experiment, and educational freedom.

What with the present rapid rate of growth in the powers of the general government, the merits of territorial democracy ought to be re-examined. A vast centralized system of national planning and benefaction is incompatible with territorial democracy. If the real powers of decision are vested in professional administrators at the nation's capital, genuine democracy—that is, the making of decisions locally and freely, by the citizens, on a humane scale—soon becomes a shadow. With it there vanishes the proliferating variety which the complex American political structure has nurtured —and that is not all which disappears.

Reasons exist why such a supplanting of prescriptive territorial democracy by a new model of central administration would present serious dangers to American order and justice and freedom I mention here only four of these.

The first is the problem of efficiency. The general government is designed to carry out certain responsibilities, fairly well defined: most notably, the conduct of foreign relations, the defense of the country, and the management of undertakings too widespread for any state to manage. But already the government in Washington is dismayingly oppressed by too much work and too many servants. Perhaps the most notorious case of federal inefficiency is that of the State Department, which has almost lost the power of decision-making because of its complexity, so that the presidents resort increasingly to personal diplomacy; the State Department already has at least one-third too many employees, countermanding each other's instructions, so that Mr. George Kennan says gloomily of this system's indigestion: "Only some form of catastrophe—natural disaster, financial collapse, or the atomic bomb" could "dismantle it or reduce it to healthier dimensions."[8] The present State Department has made it almost impossible to conduct foreign relations, and yet reform still seems distant.

Most other major activities of the Washington government are similarly oppressed with mountains of work and bad organization. Can we safely thrust upon the general government, then, immense *new* responsibilities? By endeavoring to do everything, the Washington government might end in doing nothing successfully. And ours is not a situation in which we can risk the chance of a defense establishment still less effectual than at present against the possibility, say, of eliminating rural poverty in the Ozarks by federal management.

The second is the problem of scale. Measures which the provincial governors at Graz or Innsbruck would hesitate to entrust to Vienna are proposed, in America, as if the governing of a hundred and eighty million people were little more difficult than the conduct of a town meeting—and quite as democratic, so long as president and congressmen still are elected. I have heard American advocates of social-welfare measures, for instance, seriously advance the example of social-democratic legislation in Denmark as precedent for American policy—though some American counties, not to mention states, are larger than Denmark—and other counties have more people than there are Danes.

Appeals against imprudent or unjust administration become

[8] George Kennan, "America's Administrative Response to Its World Problems," *Daedalus*, Vol. LXXXVII (Spring, 1958), p. 23.

immensely difficult when they are only the faint voices of individuals or local groups, opposed to the prestige and influence of administrators at the capital; indeed, the chief administrators themselves cannot possibly look deeply into such complaints. Detailed administration on such a scale would require from civil servants a wisdom and a goodness never experienced in human history. "Well, appeal to your congressman," the centralizers say, perhaps ingenuously. But congressmen already do not have time to answer their constituents' mail, let alone act as so many Don Quixotes of the mass state; and nearly every congressman is aghast at the prospect of becoming a redresser of grievances in every local school dispute, say.

The third difficulty I raise here is the problem of leadership. Centralized power functions smoothly only in nations accustomed to defer to the measures and opinions of a governing class—that is, in aristocratic lands. Soviet centralization would have failed altogether, had it not been for the long-established powers of the Old Regime at Moscow and St. Petersburg. And such a body of decision-makers, of governors, of aristocrats, must possess a high degree of self-confidence and the habit of command. They must be accustomed to dealing with deferential populations.

But these United States, accustomed to territorial democracy, have no class of leaders and administrators competent to undertake the consolidated direction which the centralizers propose. An English civil servant once told a member of the House of Commons that the nation would be more efficiently governed if only Parliament were swept away and the civil service given total charge of affairs. "No doubt," the M.P. replied, "and within a fortnight you would all be hanging from lamp-posts." Bagehot wrote of England as a deferential nation; and that element of deference to a class of leaders almost hereditary has not yet altogether vanished from Britain. But in America we have nothing of the sort. I think of an observation of E. L. Godkin, in 1891:

> In democratic countries [the state] represents the party which secured most votes at the last election, and is, in many cases, administered by men whom no one would make guardians of his children or trustees of his property. When I read the accounts given by the young lions of the

historical school of the glorious future which awaits us as
soon as we get the proper amount of state interference with
our private concerns for the benefit of the masses, and
remember that in New York "the state" consists of the
Albany Legislature under the guidance of Governor Hill,
and in New York City of the little Tammany junta known
as "the Big Four," I confess I am lost in amazement.[9]

Applied to Washington now, this sarcasm loses little of its force.
I do not discern a class of men competent to rule wisely this immense nation, once territorial democracy—which, by the way, is a
principal school for national office—should be undone.

Fourth, even had we a class of Winchester old-school-tie administrators, I do not know how we could expect the most expert
of statists to direct paternally and justly the concerns of this immense nation, once local volition and private self-reliance had been
seriously weakened. Any man has but twenty-four hours in his day,
and can read only a limited number of books and papers. Such
centralization defeats its own object, in persons as in departments.
The man-killing job of the presidency—to which the centralizers
would add numerous new responsibilities—may be sufficient illustra-
tion of my meaning. Professor Wilhelm Röpke puts the matter
succinctly:

> Our world suffers from the fatal disease of concentration,
> and those—the politicians, leading personalities of the
> economy, chief editors, and others—in whose hands the
> threads converge have a task which simply exceeds human
> nature. The constant strain is propagated through all other
> levels, down to the harassed foreman and his like. It is the
> curse of our age. It is a curse twice over because these men,
> who can do their duty only at the peril of angina pectoris,
> lack the time for calm reflection or the quiet reading of a
> book.[10]

Nor will this problem be alleviated by forming committees:
for committees only waste the precious time of the men who are

[9] E. L. Godkin, *Problems of Modern Democracy* (New York: Scribner,
1898), pp. 173–74.
[10] Wilhelm Röpke, *A Humane Economy* (Chicago: Henry Regnery
Company, 1959), p. 179.

expected to decide everything for everybody. The cure for paralyzing concentration, such writers as Dr. Kariel seem to argue, is greater concentration of power. This argument, to my mind, is such stuff as dreams are made of.

By way of peroration, I cannot do better than to return to Tocqueville, in his section on Townships and Municipal Bodies, where he puts with a high acuteness the case for a general "federalism," territorial democracy, of which state powers are part:

> The partisans of centralization in Europe are wont to maintain that the government can administer the affairs of each locality better than the citizens can do it for themselves. This may be true when the central power is enlightened and the local authorities are ignorant; when it is alert and they are slow; when it is accustomed to act and they to obey. Indeed, it is evident that this double tendency must augment with the increase of centralization, and that the readiness of the one and the incapacity of the others must become more and more prominent. But I deny that it is so when the people are as enlightened, as awake to their own interests, and as accustomed to reflect on them as the Americans are. I am persuaded, on the contrary, that in this case the collective strength of the citizens will always conduce more efficaciously to the public welfare than the authority of the government. I know it is difficult to point out with certainty the means of arousing a sleeping population and of giving it passions and knowledge which it does not possess; it is, I am well aware, an arduous task to persuade men to busy themselves about their own affairs. It would frequently be easier to interest them in the punctilios of court etiquette than in the repairs of their common dwelling. But whenever a central administration affects completely to supersede the persons most interested, I believe that it is either misled or desirous to mislead. However enlightened or skillful a central power may be, it cannot of itself embrace all the details of the life of a great nation. Such vigilance exceeds the powers of man. And when it attempts unaided to create and set in motion so many complicated springs, it must submit itself to a very imperfect result or exhaust itself in bootless efforts.[11]

[11] *Democracy in America,* Vol. I, pp. 89–90.

# The Prospects for Territorial Democracy in America

To destroy territorial democracy in America is quite possible—or to let it atrophy; but it is less easy to provide some alternative satisfactory scheme of politics. Once the principle of volition, with the sense of participation and local decision, vanishes from American life, Americans are liable to become an unmanageable people. On a grander and more catastrophic scale, we might see again the resistance to authority and resort to violence which were provoked by the Eighteenth Amendment and the Volstead Act. Both the Eighteenth Amendment and the Volstead Act were "democratically" adopted; but somehow national positive democracy is not the same thing as territorial prescriptive democracy.

Within a few years if not immediately, any "guided democracy" or "plebiscitary democracy" would meet with evasion and hostility immensely widespread; and among the consequences of this would come a diminishing of the really effectual and popular authority of the general government. The energies of volition would have been supplanted by the compulsions of latter-day Jacobinism. And a great big Federal Bureau of Investigation would not be able to enforce the decrees of such a regime: for though a new broom sweeps clean, and an elite federal detective force aiding the local police is one thing, a permanent national secret police would be quite another—and possibly disagreeable to some of the "liberal" advocates of centralization.

We need to recall the general distinctions among federal, state, and local governments, putting our emphasis upon the retention of vigor by state and local authorities. In our time there exists no danger that our country might fall into disunion because of "chaos" in government. (To the centralizer-on-principle, diversity and chaos are identical.) Our peril lies altogether the other way: the triumph of the total, centralized state, with the dwindling of local and private vitality, and the extinction of territorial democracy.

Yet life still rises in the tree of American federalism, and territorial democracy's powers of resistance and reaction ought not to be disregarded. It is true, as Tocqueville remarked, that men in power generally feel impelled to augment central power, while the opponents of centralization are either stupid or powerless. Notwithstanding this, attachment to the doctrines of division of authority and of state and local rights remains so popular in the United States that an intelligent plan for preserving territorial democracy would obtain a hearing, and even stand some chance of enactment.

An immense, unitary, omnipotent nation-state cannot abide territorial democracy. If the federal system is obsolete, then we ought to prepare to train the leaders of a new order, and to define the character of that domination, novel to us. If territorial democracy deserves to live, then the federal arrangement ought to be buttressed and helped to perform its functions. At present, most of the Americans qualified to think about such matters decline to take either of these courses.

Herbert J. Storing

•

# THE PROBLEM OF BIG GOVERNMENT

"Big government" is widely considered to be one of the most serious
threats to the preservation of cherished American institutions and
values. Government constantly takes on new functions and scarcely
ever abandons an old one; it grows increasingly centralized, complex,
and remote. Somewhere the old idea of a limited government of
limited powers seems to have been lost sight of, and the loss seems
to have to do with two diseases infecting political life in the United
States today: the stifling of the states by the imperialistic expansion
of the national government and the growth of an enormous, irresponsible bureaucracy.

Deploring the tendency "to further centralize problems and
their attempted solutions in the National Government rather than
to leave them to proper State and local treatment," the president
of the Chamber of Commerce told a committee of the House of
Representatives a few years ago that "there is hardly anyone who
will not agree that the basic intent of the founders of the Constitution regarding federalism has been distorted over the years."[1] The
"basic intent of the founders" is indeed the place to begin, although
we may find it necessary to go beyond their intent regarding federalism in order to understand federalism itself. That is not to say that
we must accept uncritically the opinions of the Founders or that we
should expect to find in them the whole solution to present problems.
We shall need to investigate not only the intention of the Founders
but also the reasons that lay behind that intention; we shall need to
examine not only the machinery of government which they devised

[1] Hearings before a Subcommittee of the Committee on Government
Operations, *Federal-State-Local Relations,* 85th Congress, 1st session, 1958,
pp. 52–53.

but also the principles upon which that machinery was based. Those principles give our government its enduring character, and it is with them that an understanding of our modern problem of big government must begin.

In considering the intention of the framers of the Constitution it is of the greatest importance to understand that they deliberately chose a strong national government. The most persistent argument of those who opposed the Constitution was directed against that great decision; and even some of the defenders of "big government" accepted it reluctantly and fearfully and urged that the powers of the national government be cautiously granted and prudently hedged. Consequently much of the discussion at the time of the framing and ratification of the Constitution was about whether the national government should be a little more or a little less powerful, whether the line between it and the state governments should be drawn a little higher here, a little lower there. No man could then, or can today, ignore the multitude of contingencies that must affect the apportionment of powers in particular cases or fail to recognize that these are judgments about which even sober and wise men may disagree; but wise men will try to form their judgments in the light of enduring principle. What were the principles underlying the decision for a strong national government? By examining briefly the views of some of those Founders who distinguished themselves by their share in the decision and their understanding of its significance, we can perceive several distinct but connected levels of the argument that found expression in the Constitution, each of which retains an immediate relevance to federalism today.

All past history seemed to many Americans in 1787 to show that no republican government could cover an area as large as the thirteen states and their adjacent territories. Only in a very small country, many contended, is it possible to foster that self-sacrificing devotion to the public interest, that pervasive patriotic spirit, and that close scrutiny of government officials by the people which are essential to the maintenance of freedom. It is the states, Luther Martin argued in the Constitutional Convention, to which the people look "for the security of their lives, liberties and properties"; the

# The Problem of Big Government

federal government was formed for the limited purpose of defending the whole against foreign enemies and the smaller states against the greater.[2] This view of the American Union suffered from at least one obvious defect. Most of the American states were already considerably larger than the small republics to which the defenders of state authority alluded. Referring to Montesquieu's influential argument that popular government can exist only in a small territory, Alexander Hamilton pointed out that

> the standards he had in view were of dimensions, far short of the limits of almost every one of these States. . . . If we therefore take his ideas on this point, as the criterion of truth, we shall be driven to the alternative, either of taking refuge at once in the arms of monarchy, or of splitting ourselves into an infinity of little jealous, clashing, tumultuous commonwealths, the wretched nurseries of unceasing discord and the miserable objects of universal pity or contempt.[3]

Even in their own states Americans were committed to a form of popular government on a far larger scale than the small republics of theory or of classical antiquity.

Hamilton also attacked the accepted view of confederation, and the inferences drawn from it, from the other side. The Articles of Confederation, in one view, constituted a league principally concerned with the most primitive of political objectives: defense. A substantial part of Hamilton's argument in *The Federalist* papers (where safety against foreign arms and influence is the first subject treated) is devoted to showing that even that very limited but primary and universally accepted end requires a real government with very substantial powers. "States," Patrick Henry told the Virginia Ratifying Convention, "are the characteristics and the soul of a confederation."[4] Hamilton showed (and Henry agreed) that

[2] Max Farrand (ed.), *The Records of the Federal Convention* (rev. ed.; New Haven: Yale University Press, 1937), Vol. I, pp. 340–41 (June 20).

[3] *The Federalist* 9. Quotations are taken from the edition of Jacob E. Cooke (Middletown, Conn.: Wesleyan University Press, 1961).

[4] Jonathan Elliot, *The Debates in the Several State Conventions on the Adoption of the Federal Constitution* (2nd ed.; Washington, 1836), Vol. III, p. 22.

the Constitution was based on a decisive rejection of that first principle of confederation. Under the Articles of Confederation, whose Congress depended on the states both for its sustenance and for the execution of its commands, we had "neither troops nor treasury nor government."[5] The Articles were an attempt to provide the benefits of government through the instrumentality of a league; but only government, an effective controlling authority, can provide the benefits of government. Moreover, the needs of defense and diplomacy cannot be predicted in advance, because they will be largely determined by other nations. "The circumstances that endanger the safety of nations are infinite; and for this reason no constitutional shackles can wisely be imposed on the power to which the care of it is committed."[6] If out of cowardice or parsimony such shackles are imposed, either they will prove fatal to the defense of the Union against unscrupulous enemies or they will be violently broken under the strain of necessity.

Define the powers of the national government and apportion the different objects of government between the nation and the states "as far as it can be done," Hamilton said; but let us have no mean cheeseparing in giving the national government its powers. The limited character of the national government established by the Constitution, important as that is, is subordinate to the fact that it *is* a national government. "For the absurdity must continually stare us in the face of confiding to a government, the direction of the most essential national interests, without daring to trust it with the authorities which are indispensable to their proper and efficient management. Let us not attempt to reconcile contradictions, but firmly embrace a rational alternative."[7] The congenital and fatal contradiction in the argument of the Anti-Federalists (and of their heirs throughout American history) lay in their unwillingness either to abandon a national government to protect national interests (to adopt, that is to say, a purely federal arrangement) or to entrust that national government with the authority necessary to accomplish its ends.

To this it might be replied that an illogical argument is not

[5] *The Federalist* 15.
[6] *Ibid.* 23; cf. 30, 31, 34.
[7] *Ibid.* 23.

necessarily an impolitic one. Some of the opponents of the Constitution, like Patrick Henry, feared, not without reason, that the tendency of Hamilton's cold logic was to expand the primary objective of defense into something of a less modest character. "You are not to inquire how your trade may be increased," Henry thundered to the Virginia Ratifying Convention, "nor how you are to become a great and powerful people, but how your liberties can be secured; for liberty ought to be the direct end of your government." "If we admit this consolidated government, it will be because we like a great, splendid one."[8] Some form of federation is indeed necessary, it was admitted, but the emphasis ought to be on the small republican units, where liberty is at home. If there is a tension between the safety of the Union and individual liberty, it is at least arguable (although, not surprisingly, it is seldom argued openly) that it is preferable to risk the former rather than the latter. If the Anti-Federalists neither resolved what was very widely seen as the dilemma of the American confederation nor accepted Hamilton's resolution, at least they continued to cling, as hard as they could, to the other horn.

James Madison's great contribution to the defense of the Constitution, during and after the Convention, was his powerful and influential effort to resolve this dilemma by transcending it, by showing the inadequacy of the Anti-Federalists argument, not only on the ground of the needs of the Union, but on their own chosen ground of the preservation of individual liberty.[9] Madison was of course committed to popular government as the surest means to that end which all Americans regarded, with Jefferson, as the end of government, to secure the inalienable rights of men. But he argued

---

[8] Elliot, *Debates,* Vol. III, pp. 44–45, 53.

[9] See especially Farrand, *Records,* Vol. I, pp. 134–36, 421–23 (June 6, June 26); Letter to Thomas Jefferson, October 24, 1787; and *The Federalist* 10.

In view of a popular opinion that the multiple authorship of *The Federalist* papers resulted in an argument which has a "split personality," it should be said that, although the authors are identified separately in this essay and although they sometimes make *different* arguments, there is no *inconsistency* in their arguments presented here. Specifically, whatever their differences on other questions and at other times, there was no substantial difference between Hamilton and Madison on the subject of federalism, or the relation of the nation and the states, at the time of the Founding.

(what would also have been widely accepted) that popular government faces one great danger to which all popular governments of former times had succumbed, namely, the tendency of the mass of the people to form unjust combinations against the few. Within the cramped confines of a small state, where economic opportunities are narrow and the number of different interests small, the line between rich and poor is likely to become sharply defined and ominously rigid—and when the many combine, the liberties of all are in peril. Only a large and rich territory under a single government can provide that diversity and opportunity by means of which the elemental conflict of rich and poor may be softened and diffused.[10]

What is significant about this argument for our present purposes is that the states do not in principle play any necessary part in it. (The tenth *Federalist* is a discussion of the principle of the enlargement of the orbit of republican government in its application to a single unit of government.) Madison does not accept the view that the American Union is fundamentally a kind of tension or balance between the general and the particular governments. The federal features of the system established by the Constitution, including the federal features of the central government itself were indeed a practical necessity; and, providing they do not get out of hand, they contribute a useful additional basis of fragmentation and mutual check. But they are not essential. And because they are not essential, their necessity and usefulness depend on a wide variety of changeable circumstances.

Madison's argument rests on a doubt about the efficacy of securing liberty by relying on the moral, religious, and patriotic sentiments which were supposed to characterize the small republic. A better, or more reliable, base is a wide community of industrious men with much opportunity to gratify their private desires and little opportunity to combine unjustly with others. But even Madison's intricate net of calculation rests upon a deeper conviction about the nature of American life, a perception of the moral unity of the United States of America and, before that, of the United Colonies. Madison clearly assumes, although he does not always stress, that the platform for the release of men's private energies is some degree of public-

[10] See Martin Diamond's more extended discussion of Madison's argument in his essay in this volume.

spiritedness or patriotism, expressed at least as veneration of the Constitution.[11] The conviction of a more than expediential foundation of the Union underlies even the expediential arguments themselves. It provides the theme of the opening *Federalist* papers, as well as one necessary condition of Madison's extended republic; it was the deepest ground touched (if not fully explored) in the Constitutional Convention and is the foundation of the nationalist position. Many times challenged, often only dimly understood and articulated, this national unity—not states' rights, localism, or "territorial democracy"—is the frame of American life.

*The Federalist* opens with an elaborate defense of Union and only later proceeds to criticize the Articles of Confederation. No doubt the authors were reluctant to begin their argument with a frontal attack on what was, after all, the established government (to the extent that it was a government) of the United States; and they were conscious of the rhetorical advantage of beginning their defense of the new Constitution with a suggestion that there was a whispering campaign under way against the old Union, which almost all Americans valued. But their strategy also has a deeper significance. The Constitution aimed to form, not a new Union, but "a more perfect Union"; and in the second *Federalist* paper, John Jay sought to give expression to the common understanding of that Union. He observed "one connected, fertile, wide spreading country," which "Providence has been pleased to give ... to one united people, a people descended from the same ancestors, speaking the same language, professing the same religion, attached to the same principles of government, very similar in their manners and customs, and who, by their joint counsels, arms and efforts, fighting side by side throughout a long and bloody war, have nobly established their general Liberty and Independence." This was no League of Nations, no alliance of separate, independent communities, but a country and a people made for each other. The argument of *The Federalist,* and of the Founders generally, proceeds from and depends on a conviction that, in Jay's words, "an inheritance so proper and convenient for a band of brethren, united to each other by the strongest ties, should never be split into a number of unsocial, jealous and alien sovereignties."

---

[11] See Elliot, *Debates,* Vol. III, pp. 536–37; *The Federalist* 49.

## Herbert J. Storing

As this theme opens, so also it closes *The Federalist*'s defense of Union. In the fourteenth paper, it is Madison who warns:

> Hearken not to the unnatural voice which tells you that the people of America, knit together as they are by so many cords of affection, can no longer live together as members of the same family; can no longer continue the mutual guardians of their mutual happiness; can no longer be fellow citizens of one great respectable and flourishing empire. . . . No my countrymen, shut your ears against this unhallowed language. Shut your hearts against the poison which it conveys; the kindred blood which flows in the veins of American citizens, the mingled blood which they have shed in defence of their sacred rights, consecrate their union, and excite horror at the idea of their becoming aliens, rivals, enemies.

The debates in the Constitutional Convention turned, at one of their most interesting and crucial points, on the same view of the nature of the Union. Discussing the legal status of the states and their representatives at the Convention, Luther Martin of Maryland (later a prominent Anti-Federalist) contended that the separation from Great Britain had placed the thirteen former colonies in a state of nature toward each other, and that they would have thus remained except for the Articles of Confederation, which they had entered on a footing of equality. This was promptly denied by James Wilson of Pennsylvania, who read to the Convention the language of the Declaration of Independence, observing "that the *United Colonies* were declared to be free and independent States." This language is not unambiguous, but Wilson inferred (as, incidentally, did Orestes Brownson later) that the states were independent not individually but unitedly, and that therefore they had never been independent of one another.[12] According to Martin, then, the only relations between the states had been those of free and equal sovereigns, whether at the time of the Revolution or under the Articles of Confederation. The states were the only real governments, and the Union was their creature. Wilson, on the other hand, argued that the states had never been independent sovereigns. The Ameri-

---

[12] Farrand, *Records,* Vol. I, pp. 323–24 (June 19); cf. Orestes A. Brownson, *The American Republic* (New York: P. O'Shea, 1866), p. 210.

can Union was forged during the War of Independence and constituted by the Declaration of Independence. The Articles, far from creating the Union, were only a temporary instrument of a pre-existing Union. This instrument was defective in many respects, the most important being the admission of all states to equal suffrage; there was never an American *federation* in the old and strict sense. Wilson had stated the grounds of this argument early in the debates:

> Among the first sentiments expressed in the first Congress one was that Virginia is no more. That Massachusetts is no [more], that Pennsylvania is no more, etc. We are now one nation of brethren. We must bury all local interests and distinctions. This language continued for some time. The tables at length began to turn. No sooner were the State Governments formed than their jealousy and ambition began to display themselves. Each endeavoured to cut a slice from the common loaf, to add to its own morsel, till at length the confederation became frittered down to the impotent condition in which it now stands. . . . To correct its vices is the business of this convention. One of its vices is the want of an effectual controul in the whole over its parts. What danger is there that the whole will unnecessarily sacrifice a part? But reverse the case, and leave the whole at the mercy of each part, and will not the general interest be continually sacrificed to local interests?[13]

As is shown in other essays in this volume and as, indeed, is clear from the opening words of the Constitution, the issue was resolved in favor of the whole. As is also clear, the issue was not resolved without compromise. At each of the great crises of American history, and most of the minor ones, the issue has been raised again; each time it has been settled more decisively and with less compromise. What de Tocqueville called an "incomplete national government" is, it seems, nearly completed. Yet there is a significant ambiguity in de Tocqueville's characterization. Neither the original decision for Union—and this Union did not, after all, avoid its civil war—nor the numerous reaffirmations of this decision ensured the completion of the nation. The Constitution was imperfect, as any work of man must be; but the legal and institutional framework that it provided did point in the direction of the completion of the nation

[13] Farrand, *Records,* Vol. I, pp. 166–67 (June 8).

precisely because it **was**, as John Adams said so well, "admirably calculated" to unite the "interests and affections" of the United States, to bring them "to an uniformity of principles and sentiments," and to unite "their wills and forces as a single nation."[14] The circumstances of the birth and colonial organization of the United States led to the consequence that its great political debates have taken the form (or sometimes the guise) of debates about federalism. Perhaps federalism is no longer so relevant as it once was to the question of the completion of the American nation, as a whole and in its parts; but the issue is not whether federalism is obsolete, because the debate was never fundamentally a debate about federalism.

What has this to do with "territorial democracy," or what has "territorial democracy" to do with this? Not much. It is true that Orestes Brownson's book on *The American Republic* is centrally concerned with "the constitution of the people [of the United States] as one people, and the distinction at the same time of this one people into particular States. . . ."[15] Brownson conducts an elaborate exploration of the problem of unity and diversity in political life and, specifically, the problem of the one and the many in American political life. American democracy he describes as "territorial democracy," an expression of "the political truth that, though the people are sovereign, it is the organic, not the inorganic people, the territorial people, not the people as simple population. . . ."[16] "Territorial democracy" stands between two extreme or corrupt forms of democracy, pure individualism, on the one hand, and pure humanitarianism or socialism, on the other hand. "Territorial democracy" also stands between two extreme and mistaken notions of the American Republic, the one stressing its fundamental diversity, the other its fundamental unity.

Now to understand Brownson's notion of "territorial democracy" would require a careful examination of his whole system of political and theological principles. No such examination is provided

[14] *A Defence of the Constitutions of Government of the United States of America* (London, 1794), Vol. III, pp. 505–06.
[15] Brownson, *The American Republic*, p. 245.
[16] *Ibid.*, pp. 10–11.

anywhere in this volume. Professor Kirk, while repeating the incantation, "territorial democracy," and commending certain ideas loosely associated with this phrase, apparently does not accept the whole of Brownson's theory. Yet he does not say which parts of his chief authority are retained and which cast out, or how anything that can be identified with Brownson remains, once "territorial democracy" is emptied of principles that Brownson thought essential to it. Consider: Brownson's study is explicitly based, as Professor Kirk's is not, upon the theological foundations of Roman Catholicism and is directed especially, although not exclusively, to Catholics. Brownson rejects, what Professor Kirk seems to accept, the political philosophy of the Founding Fathers. Brownson denies, what both the Founders and Professor Kirk assert, that the American system is one of checks and balances. Brownson denies, what the Founders and apparently also Professor Kirk assert, the conventional origin of the government; Brownson's notion of territorial democracy is an inseparable part of his theory (going far beyond anything dreamed by Jay, for example) of the Providential constitution of the United States. When to all this is added the fact that Brownson joins the Founders in denying, what Professor Kirk asserts, that the parts of the American Union have priority over the whole and that the Constitution was an act of voluntary association of territorial democracies, it becomes evident that the meaning of "territorial democracy" as it is used in the present discussion cannot and apparently is not even intended to be found in the thought of Orestes Brownson.[17]

Yet Brownson's vision of the American Republic does contain a rule that is relevant to the present discussion. Brownson states the principle upon which authority is (or ought to be) divided between the general and the particular governments as follows: "The line that distinguishes the two governments is that which distinguishes the general relations and interests from the particular relations and interests of the people of the United States."[18] On the basis of this principle, Brownson takes a very narrow view of the powers of the

[17] See *ibid.*, chs. 1, 7, 9, 10, 11, 15, *passim;* Orestes Brownson, *Selected Essays*, Introduction by Russell Kirk (Gateway Editions; Chicago: Henry Regnery Co., 1955), pp. 128–30, 161–90.
[18] Brownson, *The American Republic*, p. 255.

general government, holding, for example, that it had no constitutional power to pass the Missouri Compromise or to establish the United States Bank, and that it cannot constitutionally naturalize foreigners or impose a protective tariff. If we follow the deductions that Brownson makes from his general principle, we are bound to hold that most of the domestic activities of the national government today are unconstitutional. And the significance of such a holding would be that the question we face is not whether to preserve "territorial democracy," but whether to try to restore it, thereby overthrowing at least a century's history in an attempt to revive what, on this line of argument, cannot seriously be thought still to have the breath of life.

There is another possibility, however, and that is to accept Brownson's principle, to recognize the elusive and contingent character of any practical expression of the distinction between the general and the particular and the public and the private, and to make our own judgments as wisely and prudently as we can. If protection against crime is not a general public problem; if the problems of securing rights of individual expression, rights of privacy, and decent standards of public communication are not questions of general interest; if the quality of public education is a matter that affects individuals or citizens only in their private and domestic relations—if these are not matters of common concern, then the national government has no business meddling with them. But there is nothing in the Constitution, or in the principles of American federalism, or in the history of American government that predetermines the answer to questions such as these. In this respect Alexander Hamilton is distinctive only in the force and clarity with which he gives expression to the authentic voice of the Founders and of every responsible American statesman since that time: it is impossible to define and confine in advance the matters that may be of national concern, and the American Constitution provides, as any viable constitution must, for the exercise of national power commensurate with national exigency. The burden of proof does not lie with the advocates of strong national government but with its opponents.

That the states are not in any fundamental sense the small intimate communities of self-governing men, beloved of the heirs of Jeffersonian democracy, is surely even clearer today than it was when Hamilton pointed it out. It is difficult to see in the state governments of Tennessee or New York or Michigan much of those qualities of "local liberty," "self-government," and "democracy" with which, in the lore of federalism, the states are supposed to be associated. Tocqueville's much cited description of local government and administration[19] referred to *state* governments, where centralization has gone about as far as it has in Washington; so that school boards, for example, are much less numerous than they once were, as a result of consolidation by state governments, and are severely restricted in their discretion over curriculum, personnel, and finance, as a result of growing regulation by state departments of education. And if it is the local and municipal governments that are to be fostered as the loci of participation and intelligent concern for the public good, then it follows, in the first place, that it is not a problem of federalism or "territorial democracy," and, in the second place, that it is not wrong in principle, if it is desirable on other grounds, for the national government to deal directly with the local units and use them as administrative instruments, as the states do.

Obviously the American decision for Union had and still has its risks, required and still requires prudent implementation. To decide that a problem is one of national concern and requires national action is not necessarily to centralize the whole business of formulating and administering a program in Washington, even ignoring, as we ought not ignore, that while "Washington" is not merely the sum of its parts, neither is it a place where the states and localities are without influence. It may be conceded that a certain price was paid for Union, that there are some genuine values associated with the small community, and that one of the problems of modern American political life is to find ways of strengthening those values under conditions that are sometimes unfavorable. This does not require, or even permit, a doctrinaire commitment to a species of localism or states' rights that is even less relevant to the conditions of Union now than when it was first rejected as its governing principle. Tocqueville characterized the American system, let it be remembered, as one of centralized *government* and decentralized

[19] Alexis de Tocqueville, *Democracy in America,* ed. Phillips Bradley (New York: Knopf, 1945), Vol. I, ch. 5.

*administration.*[20] It is by no means clear whether in this respect there has been any fundamental change since Tocqueville's time, although in response to new circumstances the means of government and administration have certainly changed. In many new (as well as the old) relationships between the established governments and in a wide variety of new instruments, serious and responsible attempts have been made to bring the values of decentralized administration into centralized government. One of the interesting questions of the 1970s will be whether revenue sharing can be used to restore, or to preserve, some significant vitality in local units of government. Another will be whether the nation's school boards—themselves increasingly large bureaucracies, loosely controlled by lay boards—can discharge their responsibilities for education while also putting themselves into some significant contact with parents and other affected segments in their communities. Experience has been mixed, but it does not give much support to the idea that the schools' problems can be solved by simply "returning" them to the people. And as for the countless devices of consultation that cluster around every agency of national government, if these are sometimes ill conceived or their value grossly exaggerated—one thinks of the participation of the poor in the poverty program—do they really compare so unfavorably with the more traditional forms of local participation as means of collecting information, securing consent, providing schools of citizenship, and checking central government? Even the much criticized TVA "grass-roots democracy" and the "self-governing" committees in the agricultural program are scarcely open to a single objection that cannot equally well be directed against township, county, and state units of government and administration.

It is, moreover, important to beware of the excesses too often associated with a merely sentimental or ideological attachment to local democracy. When Madison argues that a democracy "will be confined to a small spot," while "a republic may be extended over a large region,"[21] he is not, to repeat, defending pure or simple democracy (and then trying to reconcile it with national interests);

[20] Tocqueville's distinction is similar to Brownson's, see *ibid.*, above pp. 75–76.
[21] *The Federalist* 14.

rather, he is pointing to the fundamental defect of local democracy and the way to its avoidance. Even if we did not have Madison's powerful assistance in warning us of the narrow, mean, and tyrannical aspects of the small units of republican government, we could scarcely ignore the examples that can be found in every state of the Union. Let it be conceded that it would be a national disaster if the educational system were wholly in the hands of the professional educators centered in Washington (or for that matter in the state capitals where they are now strongly entrenched), but the consequences would perhaps be only slightly less serious if the system were wholly in the hands of local school boards or local parents' groups. The Founders emphatically did not accept the idea that the best government is the government closest to the people. Their argument, on the contrary, was that one of the great defects of popular government up to that time, including many of the American states, had been that they were too close to the people, too easily infected with popular moods and fancies, too little equipped to guide the people and to resist them when the common good so demanded.

What then of the risks of strong central government? What of the dangers of "democratic centralism" or "Jacobinism" or "plebiscitary democracy"? What of the argument that today's resistance to a strong and increasingly popular national government is an extension of the original and laudable conservative defense against majority tyranny? This argument does indeed proceed from one of the main concerns of the Founders and demands serious consideration.

Let us first remind ourselves of some fundamentals. The need for government, the Founders thought, arises out of the impossibility of any real freedom without it. Under conditions of anarchy where every man is perfectly at liberty to do as he likes, every man is subject to constant fear of everyone else; and this is the meanest kind of slavery. Yet because of the tendency for any man to tyrannize over others if he gets the chance, government itself may become the source of another kind of slavery where men live in fear, not of all other men, but of that one man or small group of men who hold them in thralldom. The problem of government for the Founders, one could almost say, was to steer a course between these extremes. That is the meaning of the remark:

> If men were angels, no government would be necessary. If angels were to govern men, neither external nor internal controuls on government would be necessary. In framing a government which is to be administered by men over men, the great difficulty lies in this: You must first enable the government to controul the governed; and in the next place, oblige it to controul itself.[22]

One way of controlling the government is to establish a federal system in which the powers of government are distributed between two levels of government, but it was by no means only Alexander Hamilton who feared that too strong a draught of the federal remedy was likely to prove as bad as the tyrannical disease. In any case the Founders did not commit the absurdity of trying to control the national government by withholding from it powers necessary to the accomplishment of vital national objectives. The safeguard against tyranny and injustice was sought in a powerful national government with an *internal* composition and structure such as to render it a fit and trustworthy depository of the national interest.[23] The general principle, of course, was that it is prudent to let one governor check another. More particularly, the machinery of government should be so ordered as to provide a check against the tendency for the most popular branch of the government to concentrate power into its own hands and to become the engine of that tyranny of the majority which is fatal to liberty.

[22] *Ibid.* 51.
[23] Cf. Tocqueville, *Democracy in America,* Vol. 1, ch. 5, "Administration in New England."

John Adams' famous *Defence of the Constitutions of Government of the United States of America,* with its attack on Turgot's thesis of collecting "all authority into one center, the nation," was not a defense of federalism, has nothing to do with federalism, and was first published before the Constitutional Convention met. Convinced that "the mistakes of great men, and even the absurdities of fools" cannot be too fully refuted when they strengthen false prejudices, Adams did provide an elaborate defense of the organization of the American *state* governments and of the system of internal checks and balances on which they, and later the national government, were based. See Vol. I, Letter 2, cf., p. 46.

# The Problem of Big Government

In devising a system of checks and balances the Founders confronted two major difficulties. First, merely dividing governmental powers was not likely to provide any effective restraint if each of the separate parts were animated by the same spirit. Yet the classic English solution—a government composed of king, nobles, and commons, whose authority rested, at least partly, on different principles—was clearly unavailable to Americans, even if they had desired to utilize it. The problem was how to inform some parts of a government that was *basically* popular with a spirit that would not be *simply* popular. The second difficulty was how to prevent a government of checks and balances from reaching such a perfect equilibrium that it could not act at all. The Founders' response to both of these difficulties culminates in the presidency, an institution that, far more than federalism, represents the Founders' achievement and their challenge.

The president was to be part of the system of checks and balances and the chief counterweight to the legislative branch. But he was also to be the primary source of energy and direction for the government as a whole. To select the president, the Founders invented the electoral college system, and it is more important for the present to consider what this invention was supposed to do than to see that it did not work as expected. It was arranged to allow "the sense of the people" to operate, while leaving the immediate selection of the president to an *ad hoc* body of judicious and wise men. Under this system, Hamilton argued, "there will be a constant probability of seeing the station filled by characters pre-eminent for ability and virtue."[24] In addition, the system was designed to leave the president free from a dependence on any other branch of the government; for this was to be no subservient administrator, no timeserver, no mere doer of the will of Congress or the people. On the wisdom and courage of the president, on his capacity to guide the people when they were confused, encourage them when they were right, and stand against them—at least to demand that they think again—when they were wrong, would depend the excellence of the American government, the effectiveness of its protection of liberty, and the greatness to which it might aspire. The presidency

[24] *The Federalist* 68.

was the crucial feature of the Constitution, and in spite of many changes it remains so, because the duty of the holder of this office is the most difficult in any popular government: to reconcile the wants of the people and the needs of the Republic.

While this reconciliation was to be above all the duty of the president, the Founders provided subordinate institutions designed to the same end. Of these the Senate is especially relevant here. A smaller body than the other house of the legislature, composed of older men, and elected by the state legislatures, it was expected to be less inclined to yield to sudden and violent passions and thus to add stability and moderation to the national councils. The Senators' longer terms of office would enable them to acquire a greater understanding of "the objects and principles of legislation" and encourage them to think in terms of the long-range interest and reputation of the country. They could, when necessary, resist the excesses of the popular branch of the legislature and of the people themselves.

> As the cool and deliberate sense of the community ought in all governments, and actually will in all free governments ultimately prevail over the views of its rulers; so there are particular moments in public affairs, when the people stimulated by some irregular passion, or some illicit advantage, or misled by the artful misrepresentations of interested men, may call for measures which they themselves will afterwards be the most ready to lament and condemn. In these critical moments, how salutary will be the interference of some temperate and respectable body of citizens, in order to check the misguided career, and to suspend the blow meditated by the people against themselves, until reason, justice and truth, can regain their authority over the public mind?[25]

Today, of course, the Senate is elected directly by the people, and it is but a faint reflection of its original self. It is far more popular, far more susceptible to the passing fancies of the people, than the Founders intended. Yet the people are still sometimes ignorant, fickle, and unjust; and it remains the problem of popular government not only to protect the people against betrayal by their representatives but also to protect them, in Madison's words, "against

[25] *Ibid.* 62, 63.

the transient impressions into which they themselves might be led.[26] If the Senate today is less well adapted to this end than it was expected by the Founders to be, is there any institution in the national government that fills (or might fill) a role like that of the original Senate? I suggest that we consider—strange as it may seem—the national bureaucracy.

It is not for its "senatorial" qualities that the national bureaucracy is mainly known today, but rather for its size, complexity, unresponsiveness, and impenetrability. Hamilton, like Madison, thought that one of the advantages of the central government over the state governments was its being "more out of the reach of those occasional ill humors of temporary prejudices and propensities" which tend to infect public opinion.[27] The central government today is much less "out of reach," but the bureaucracy does to a very considerable extent (and might to a much greater extent) exercise a steady pressure upon our political leaders to transcend passing desires and prejudices. Obviously the bureaucracy is not a senate; but it may well be one of the most effective approximations to a senate that we have available today. That it has not performed its "senatorial" functions as well as it might is due in no small part to the thoughtless, irresponsible, and sometimes violent attacks to which it is so often subjected, even by those groups whose natural ally it is.

This does not mean that the bureaucracy ought to be above criticism. There is no disposition here to deny the existence of inefficiency, ignorance, cowardice, indecision, narrowness, irresponsibility, and petty tyranny in the national bureaucracy, although whether these evils are more prevalent there than in the states and localities may be doubtful. Perhaps the most serious difficulty of our huge administration, as George Kennan points out in the powerful criticism to which Professor Kirk refers, is its tendency towards "fragmentation and diffusion of power."[28] Kennan's criticism, whatever else it is, is not an argument for decentralization of *government,* of deliberation about national requirements, of responsible decisions. Quite the reverse. It is significant, moreover, that the Department

---

[26] Farrand, *Records,* Vol. I, p. 421 (June 26).

[27] *The Federalist* 27.

[28] George F. Kennan, "America's Administrative Response to Its World Problems," *Daedalus* 87 (Spring 1958): 13.

of State is selected by Professor Kirk as an outstanding example of the evils of federal bureaucracy. Even accepting his dubious contention that the State Department's loss of capacity for decision has been caused by bureaucratic complexity, the administrative difficulties in the first department of the national government were surely not created by national usurpation of local functions and are not to be overcome by any adjustment of the federal system or any revival of "territorial democracy." As for the bureaucracy generally, let us keep a sense of proportion; its difficulties, great as they are, would be only very marginally affected by any conceivable responsible program of reducing the size of the national government.

It may be, as Mr. Kennan suggests, that the problem of bureaucracy is insoluble, barring some major upheaval. This need not lead to an apathetic abandonment of attempts at improvement, although it may remind us of the sound maxim of moderation, that criticism and reform based on a blind determination to wipe away all the evils of the world—even of the bureaucracy—is likely to do more harm than good, whatever the ideological underpinnings.[29] Improvement is possible. The senior civil service recommended in 1955 by the Hoover Commission is still far from realization, but that recommendation rested on a sober recognition of the major role that the bureaucracy plays in the formulation as well as the execution of national policy. It remains a relevant and well conceived proposal for improving the organization and character of the top level of the federal bureaucracy.[30] Unquestionably, if our nation requires

---

[29] An approach to the problems of contemporary government that can criticize the transfer of many matters from the regular courts of law to administrative tribunals on the astounding ground that the latter are not governed by the "democratic process"—as if the former are—does not augur well for responsible and relevant criticism.

[30] Commission on the Organization of the Executive Branch of the Government, *Personnel and Civil Service and Task Force Report on Personnel and Civil Service* (Washington: U.S. Government Printing Office, 1955). Seymor S. Berlin, "The Federal Executive Service," *Civil Service Journal,* April-June, 1971. For discussions of the broad political role of the American civil service, see Norton Long, "Bureaucracy and Constitutionalism," *American Political Science Review,* September, 1952, and "Public Policy and Administration," *Public Administration Review,* Winter, 1954; Peter Woll, *American Bureaucracy* (New York: W. W. Norton, 1963); and my essay on "Political Parties and the Bureaucracy," in *Political Parties, U.S.A.,* ed. Robert A. Goldwin (Chicago: Rand McNally & Co., 1964).

leadership, including administrative leadership, we had better give more and deeper consideration to the education of our leaders than we have done, in which quest we shall again return to the ways of the Fathers. Nor is training in "management," supplemented by short courses in "executive development," going to be enough. What is required is a higher civil service provided with not only the skills but also the political understanding and the moral character demanded by the duties thrust upon it by the modern republic. Perhaps the most serious shortcoming of the American civil service lies in its primarily technical competence and character. But random carping or wholesale condemnation of the bureaucracy has only the effect (when it has any effect) of diverting attention from the need to nurture and strengthen its capacity for administrative statesmanship and of weakening what is a prime source of intelligence as well as a major stabilizing and moderating force in American government today.

The bureaucracy is today's manifestation of the original decision for big government. Whether it is to be more a force for good than for evil depends, in the first place, on a recognition and acceptance of the fact that it is, in any case, a major force in American political life. It will not melt under the heat of fulmination or blow away on the wind of wish.

Viewed from the standpoint of the Founders, American government today seems to have been turned on its head. Generally speaking, and contrary to the Founders' expectation, it is in the state governments that the conservative and propertied interests find their main influence and support. It is the national government that seems most susceptible to pressures from the people at large and least concerned to protect the interests of the few. There lies the irony of the use by the president of the Chamber of Commerce of the Jeffersonian argument that "that government which is best for the people is that which is closest to them."[31] The state governments may be closer to the Chambers of Commerce, but today it is the national government that in all fundamental respects is closer to the people. Indeed the national government, including the Senate and the Supreme Court,

[31] Hearings, *Federal-State-Local Relations*, 1958, p. 53.

seems to have been infused with the popular spirit. And although the president is still obliged to reconcile popular wants and national needs, he has to do so today as a great popular leader rather than as one chosen by a small group of judicious men.

Some argue, therefore, that when conservatives depart from the conception of American government held by their forebears they are only adjusting themselves to new circumstances while remaining true to the traditional end, namely, to support and defend those institutions of government most closely connected with the "temperate and respectable" elements. If the Democracy has occupied the national government and the presidency, perhaps the party of the Republic must make its stand in the states and, when it can, in Congress.

This argument is untenable for two reasons. First, in seeking to strengthen state governments at the expense of the national, it demands an attitude toward American government that is not only contrary to the best conservative tradition but hopelessly unrealistic. It amounts to a permanent commitment to a series of rear-guard actions in which there is room only for retreat. Only yesterday many men insisted that social security, agricultural policy, and labor relations were purely local matters, and they sought to enforce this opinion with constitutional shackles on the national government. The effect was only to deprive those men of any influence in deciding how the nation would meet what were manifestly national problems. A rigid insistence today that such matters as unemployment, education, and the condition of our cities are not national problems will have the same kind of consequence. Our modern advocates of localism, under whatever name, may well ponder Hamilton's warning that "nations pay little regard to rules and maxims calculated in their very nature to run counter to the necessities of society. Wise politicians will be cautious about fettering the government with restrictions, that cannot be observed. . . ."[32] To strengthen, on the other hand, those qualities of the bureaucracy that contribute knowledge and moderation to government and set an example of devotion to the public good is to defend an old position with a new institution and one that runs in harmony with the "necessities of society" today.

[32] *The Federalist* 25.

# The Problem of Big Government

Second, this argument in favor of weakening the national government fails to recognize that, while a government ought to be ordered so that it will not act badly, it must also and preeminently have the capacity to act well. Just as the dangers that the nation may face are illimitable, so are its opportunities. Hamilton always kept in mind (nor did Jefferson ignore) those moments in the life of every nation when it faces great crises and great opportunities, when its course and character may be decisively influenced. And while the decent operation of government from day to day is served by a plurality of interests, by divided government, and by checks on ambition, the times of crisis and greatness demand unity and power and leadership. A constitution should so far as possible provide for both. Checks and balances are still important, and let there be no misunderstanding: decentralization of administration, a continued and even increased emphasis on state and local government where that is possible, and internal checks on ill-conceived action are legitimate and necessary. But conservatives defeat their own purposes when they set themselves against an adequate national government and a strong president and administration just because the popular elements are for them. They do no service to themselves or to the Republic when they adopt a policy of strengthening those elements of the American governmental system whose tendency is to emphasize the separateness of the parts at the expense of those in whose hands it lies to maintain the unity of the whole.

# James Jackson Kilpatrick

•

# THE CASE FOR "STATES' RIGHTS"

> What has destroyed the liberty and the rights of man in every government which has ever existed under the sun? The generalizing and concentrating all cares and powers into one body, no matter whether of the autocrats of Russia or France, or of the aristocrats of a Venetian Senate.
>
> —THOMAS JEFFERSON
> *to Joseph C. Cabell (1816)*

It offers a small footnote to the semantic confusion of our times that an essayist, assigned to prepare "the case for States' rights," must begin by saying that he does not propose to talk about States' rights. The States have very few rights. They have a right to equal representation in the United States Senate, and they have a right to be protected against invasion; but by and large, as the Ninth and Tenth Amendments make clear in their perfect choice of nouns, people have rights; States have powers. We may go a step further, and remark that today the people have fewer rights and the States have smaller powers than they possessed at one time, and we shall not be far from the mark in surmising that the cause of the former is an effect of the latter.

I would express certain convictions at the outset. Government, it seems to me, ought always to be seen clearly for what it is: A necessary evil. And the more it is thought to be necessary, the more it is bound to become evil. I do not use "evil" here to mean debauched or corrupt, though I believe such a charge could be maintained. I mean rather that government feeds upon the storehouse of man's freedom, and the more this precious granary is drawn down and nibbled away, the less remains to sustain us. I hold that all governments are oppressive: they are distinguished only by this, that some are more oppressive than others. When I am told that our government, among all the powers of the earth, is the most free, I am minded to say that it is merely the least despotic.

From what little I can read of history, and what I can perceive of our own day, I conclude that man always has existed in a condition of conflict with the state. It is inherent in the nature of man, whose first impulse is to act; it is inherent in the nature of the state, whose first duty is to restrain. A long time ago, when he was writing more poetically than politically, Jefferson put it down that governments exist to secure those unalienable rights that do indeed comprise man's inheritance here on earth—the rights to life, liberty, and the pursuit of happiness. But it has not worked out that way. In practice, governments frequently have secured our rights by judiciously taking them away, and acts of injustice to the individual have won easy sanction in the name of the common good. Let any friend of liberty read the Supreme Court's recent decisions in the Baltimore and Dayton sanitation cases, and ask himself if the citizen's right to be free from unreasonable searches and seizures has here been secured.

The chief problem of government in a free society is to keep this conflict between man and the state, the one pulling, the other hauling, under some sort of effective control, so that society moves forward and men find slight disposition to chafe under the restraints put upon them. All governments must preserve law and order; national governments must provide for the common defense. Beyond those essentials, we advance with less sureness. A large function of government is to promote the general welfare; and it is here that those of us who are styled as inexactly "conservatives" as we are mistakenly termed "States' righters" would plead for caution. "I am not a friend to very energetic government," Jefferson once remarked to Madison. "It is always oppressive."

The great men who long ago preceded us in this inquiry comprehended this conflict, this tension, with perfect clarity. They did not view the central government, as it is the custom to view it in the United States today, as a firm but loving paterfamilias, or in a less elegant image, as a comfortable sow with a hundred million teats. "Free government is founded in jealousy and not in confidence," cried the Kentucky Resolution. The authors of that Resolution had gazed upon the face of tyranny and knew it well; in forming

# The Case for "States' Rights"

their own free Republic, they brought to the creative act the accumulated wisdom of the great men who had preceded them. They *knew,* in a deep way that contemporary political philosophers do not seem to know, the conditions that historically have contributed to greatness in nations and to happiness in man. The examples of Babylonia and Greece and Rome were fresh and and commanding precepts for the delegates who met that summer in Philadelphia. It is impossible to pursue their deliberations, or to read the debates of the ratifying conventions that followed thereafter in the States, without developing a profound respect for the wisdom, the intelligence, and the sure sense of history that imbued the men who conceived our form of union. It was a small assembly that wrote the Constitution, Tocqueville observed, but it contained "the finest minds and the noblest characters that had ever appeared in the New World."[1]

In that just appraisal lies the first argument I would make in behalf of "the case for States' rights." Truly there were giants in our earth in those days. We ought to honor them. By what presumptions—by what giddy conceit—do today's political scientists, uneducated editors, witless politicians, and other ignorami assert a superior wisdom? I travel to Washington with some frequency, and I gaze from the House galleries at the awesome scene below. A few good men excepted, it offers only a milling gaggle of chiropractors, foot doctors, country clowns, elevated plumbers, and second-rate lawyers—and these, God save the mark, are the statesmen who would discard the charter of our liberties! When a mood of flagellation comes over me, and the *Congressional Record* is not at hand, I read some of the learned quarterlies and other leaf-rakings from the academic grove. These are not as funny as the *Record,* but they are more pompous and arrogant; and I recall Burke's biting comment upon the literary men, politicians, and gauzy divines who encouraged the French Revolution:

> They have no respect for the wisdom of others; but they pay it off by a very full measure of confidence in their own. With them it is a sufficient motive to destroy an old scheme of things, because it is an old one. As to the new, they are in no sort of fear with regard to the duration of a building

[1] Alexis de Tocqueville, *Democracy in America* (New York: Vintage, 1954), Vol. I, p. 118.

93

run up in haste; because duration is no object to those who think little or nothing has been done before their time, and who place all their hopes in discovery. They conceive, very systematically, that all things which give perpetuity are mischievous, and therefore they are at inexpiable war with all establishments.[2]

For my own part, I should like to remain decently obedient to Aristotle's counsel, in *Politics* (Book II), not to disregard the experience of ages. Jefferson, Mason, and Henry, to name but three of Virginia's forebears, dealt in eternal verities; to the surpassing truth of their repeated warnings against excessive centralism, our own busy philosophers have responded with no more than a few evasive falsehoods. It is said that times have changed, and the world has become smaller, and time has been telescoped into some remarkable units known as "short hours" or "short years." It is said that the dangers to the survival of civilization have become much greater. And on the broad subject of expanding government, we are told disarmingly, and in a sort of folksy grammar, that we have nothing to fear from big government for government, after all, is nobody but us.

To these familiar rationalizations, I say, nonsense! *Plus ça change, plus c'est la même chose.* Now we fly to London in five or six of those short hours; we converse by satellites that circle the globe; tomorrow the inanities of television will be bounced from the moon. But let us not be deceived into supposing that the traveler's journey is different, or that the human heart speaks in a new way, or that the old immutable laws of political behavior can be summarily amended or repealed. There is a sea change that comes over men raised from private life to public office, and if this is most clearly observed in Federal judges, it is manifest in other magistrates also. They become a part of that vast, shapeless, formless, ectoplasmic mass known as *government,* and they find themselves—even the good men—aligned in an antithetical relationship: the governed, and the governors. If this relationship normally is pleasant and benevolent, if government accomplishes much that is, provisionally, good, the abuses of power remain a constant threat. Governments exist, Cal-

[2] Edmund Burke, *Reflections on the Revolution in France* (Chicago: Regnery, 1955), p. 127.

houn observed, to restrain men; and therefore we have constitutions, to restrain governments.

Our Fathers comprehended these elementary truths; they mastered their lessons in a contemplative period when public leaders had priceless assets we deny our public men today: time to think, time to read, time to watch the seasons from a mountaintop in Albemarle. The last book I happened to put aside, of a recent afternoon, was a volume of Jefferson's letters: the first book I happened to pick up after dinner was Harry Truman's autobiography; and I was impressed, as any man must be, by the thought of how far we have advanced from Monticello—advanced, that is to say, as southerners speak of their army in the last days of the Confederacy, to the rear.

Plainly, it is not enough merely to honor the Founding Fathers for their amazing genius, or to observe with Burke that men who lose respect for their ancestors are likely to command none from their posterity. Coming closer to the point, and this is my second contention, I submit that we should respect their political handiwork also. The Constitution is not without fault; some of its provisions are archaic, and some of its language is ambiguous, and needs have developed—as Washington and Jefferson foresaw—for some desirable amendments. But it is still the supreme law of the land. We ought to obey it implicitly. And both in its basic provisions, and in the underlying political philosophy these provisions reflect, the Constitution remains to this day what Tocqueville termed it, "the most perfect federal constitution that ever existed."[3]

Even the briefest examination into these basic provisions, in terms of the case for States' rights, will disclose certain political truths the high priests of centralization cannot exorcise by the sweet smoke of pedantry. Our Union was formed by the States, acting as States; all political powers exercised by the central government come by delegation from the States; the States alone have inherent powers, while the central government has none—save those it has assumed by usurpation. If the structure of our government ever is to be altered in any essential respect, the States will have to do it. This ultimate sovereign power—"the will to enact, the power to execute," as John

[3] *Democracy in America*, Vol. I, p. 172.

Taylor of Caroline termed it—resides finally with the States. If the Union ever were to be dissolved, it would be as a consequence of State action; and the States would survive.

The objective student of the Constitution who undertakes to read our charter in terms of the State and central government relationship may be astonished at what he finds. Before he is well launched into Article I, he is brought up short by the fact that members of the House of Representatives are chosen not "by the people," but by "the people of the several States." The lower chamber was intended to represent people by the numbers, but the notable fact is that no congressional district stretches across a State line. These districts are fixed by State authority.

Who are these "people of the several States" who are to elect the Representatives? What authority fixes their qualifications to vote? Why, plainly, "the electors in each State shall have the qualifications requisite for electors of the most numerous branch of the State legislature." What of a candidate for the House? He must be at least twenty-five years old; he must have been at least seven years a citizen—but to these fairly universal standards, one more is added: He must be an inhabitant of that State "in which" he shall be chosen.

I put "in which" in quotation marks in order to emphasize a subtle but significant distinction that appears in the following section as to Senators. A Senator must be at least thirty; he must have been nine years a citizen; and he must be an inhabitant of that State "for which" he shall be chosen. The deliberate choice of prepositions points up both the equality of States and the role of Senators. Until the unfortunate adoption of the Seventeenth Amendment in 1913, Senators were chosen by State legislatures and served in effect as State ambassadors. And thinking rapidly over half a century of Senate history, I am inclined to believe the great Senators since 1913 most likely would have been named by their State legislatures if the Seventeenth Amendment never had been adopted; the senatorial mediocrities, for the most part, have been second-raters who owed their election to a gift for gab and never would have made it without the process of popular election.

Pursuing the constitutional provisions as to States, one finds the entire Constitution strung upon a thread of State responsibilities and restraints. The very words "State" or "States" appear more than ninety times; the word "nation," in reference to the United States of America, never appears at all. Our Republic three times is referred to as "this Union" and once as "the land," but every other reference is simply to "the United States"—and the proper noun is always treated as a plural noun.

The longer one reflects upon the Constitution, and upon the writings of the Founding Fathers, the more apparent two political truths become. The first deals with the source of political power; the second deals with the restraints upon power. The advocate of "States' rights" would like to be heard on both of them.

It is astonishing how many persons in public life never have grasped—or even thought about—the origin and abiding location of political power in the United States. This power now flows from fifty identical springs, filling fifty separate but identical reservoirs. And whatever powers may be vested, now or hereafter, in the central government, these powers must flow upward from the State reservoirs. The flow never goes the other way. If beginning students of the Constitution were asked to understand one truth only of their government, they could not do better than to begin with this: *The Constitution acts upon the States in a prohibitory fashion only.*

This is not true of the Constitution's action upon the central government. The Constitution both authorizes the central government to do certain things, and prohibits the central government from doing certain things, but at no point does the Constitution authorize or permit the States to do anything. As a consequence, members of the Congress embarking upon some legislative scheme must ask themselves two questions: (1) Are we permitted to do this under the Constitution? and (2) Are we prohibited from doing this under the Constitution? The States have no such problems. They have all powers to begin with. Their search is for a prohibition only, and if they find nothing *in the Constitution* prohibiting them from a particular course of action, they are free to proceed.

The Tenth Amendment makes this clear beyond peradventure. It is the key that unlocks every mystery of our form of government; it is the very polar star of our fundamental charter. "The powers [let us note the noun] not delegated [let us note the verb] to the United States by the Constitution [let us pause especially upon that

97

prepositional phrase], nor prohibited by it [the antecedent of "it" is "Constitution"] to the States, are reserved to the States respectively [there is profound meaning in that adverb] or to the people."

Why was this amendment demanded, in New Hampshire no less than in Virginia, in Rhode Island no less than in South Carolina? The object was to give expression to the underlying philosophy of the people on whom this Constitution was to act directly. *They meant to restrain.* They knew, as Jefferson remarked, that "the natural progress of things is for liberty to yield and government to gain ground," and they hoped to create a government that would gain as little such ground as possible. Thus, it will be observed that the Constitution is in many ways a very negative document. Wherever there is a giving, there is almost always a snatching back; the whole instrument abounds in "noes," "nots," "neithers," and "nors." The list of prohibitions flatly imposed upon the central government is long, but when the framers had finished their work, the States found the list not yet long enough, so they added ten broad amendments more. The prohibitions imposed by the States upon their own exercise of power, especially in the tenth section of Article I, are scarcely less impressive.

This self-evident desire to restrain *all* government pervades the entire document. Ours was to be a *limited* government. That was the whole reason the framers enumerated the powers vested in the Congress, with such tedious care that the power to punish counterfeiting is separated from the power to coin money, and the power to support an army is not joined by even a conjunction to the power to maintain a navy. Here every separate sentence is numbered; every particular power is spelled out. And what a mockery it is of their prudent labors to see men contend for the absurd notion that the power to lay taxes "to provide for the general welfare" vests the Congress with the power to do whatever Congress pleases! Such a construction reduces the Constitution to blank paper; it arrogates to judges and to congressmen the bumptious authority claimed by Humpty-Dumpty, to whom words meant what he chose them to mean, and neither more nor less. If all powers were delegated to the central government, then none remained exclusively with the States; the bulk of the Constitution is mere surplusage, and the Tenth Amendment is a fraud; the authors of *The Federalist* were

# The Case for "States' Rights"

masters of deceit, and the written English language is become the babble of idiots. Yet these are the ends the advocates of centralization would put upon us: the reversal of the flow of power, the up-ending of our structure, so that the foundation is on top and the gables down below; they would have us abandon the restraints and limitations that long ago were laid upon the States by the States themselves, and imposed on their central government by their own joint action.

Now, all of this is not to suggest that the United States do not comprise a "nation." Of course they do. Neither is it to suggest that some sharp line always has separated the powers delegated from the powers reserved. From the beginning, there has been a blurring and a mixing; the popular image of two governmental spheres, each rotating perfectly in its own separate orbit, touching but never over-lapping, has nothing in history to commend it. Nevertheless, the dual structure remains, and a full understanding of this concept is imperative to any understanding of how our Republic functions.

"The people of the United States constitute one nation, under one government, and this government, *within the scope of the powers with which it is invested,* is supreme," wrote Chief Justice Chase in 1868. "On the other hand, the people of each State comprise a State, having its own government, and endowed with all the functions essential to separate and independent existence. *The States disunited might continue to exist. Without the States in union, there could be no such political body as the United States.*"

Notice Chase's careful qualification: The central government is supreme "within the scope of the powers with which it is invested." And whence came this investiture? Not from the people in one great body. The powers of the central government, as Madison pointed out in the Virginia Convention of 1787, came from "the people as composing thirteen sovereignties." That is to say, the powers came from the States.

Yet a statement of this truth implies no hostility to a strong national government. The Federal government is our government; we owe obedience and allegiance to it. The plan of our Fathers, and it was a good plan, was simply to assure the people the best of both worlds—a central government strong enough to act boldly and powerfully in the preservation of national security and in the promotion of truly national interests, yet not so strong that it would swallow up the administration of those local and domestic responsibilities which the people wanted kept close at hand.

Tocqueville put it simply. The federal system was created, he observed, "with the intention of combining the different advantages which result from the magnitude and the littleness of nations," and he went on to describe these advantages as he perceived them in America:

> In great centralized nations the legislator is obliged to give a character of uniformity to the laws, which does not always suit the diversity of customs and of districts; as he takes no cognizance of special cases, he can only proceed upon general principles; and the population are obliged to conform to the requirements of the laws, since legislation cannot adapt itself to the exigencies and the customs of the population, which is a great cause of trouble and misery. This disadvantage does not exist in confederations; Congress regulates the principal measures of the national government, and all the details of the administration are reserved to the provincial legislatures. One can hardly imagine how much this division of sovereignty contributes to the well-being of each of the States that compose the Union.[4]

At a later point, I want to touch upon the troubles that arise when the central government ceases to heed "the diversity of customs and of districts." Here I would dwell a little longer upon the political insight, as I conceive it, that went into the structure of our government. The Founding Fathers wanted not only to restrain all governments. *They wanted also to preserve that sense of close community which is the starting point of political well-being.* Burke, in his *Reflections on the Revolution in France,* put it this way: "To be attached to the subdivision, to love the little platoon we belong to in society, is the first principle (the germ as it were) of public affections. It is the first link in the series by which we proceed towards a love to our country, and to mankind."[5]

Let that sense of community be dulled or lost, and something precious is abandoned. Let local powers atrophy, and State pre-

[4] *Democracy in America,* Vol. I, pp. 168–69.
[5] Pp. 71–72.

rogatives decline, and the wellspring of patriotism inevitably must run thin. For this sense of community, unless it is nurtured at home, cannot flourish and retain its simple vitality in a "community" that stretches from Maine to Hawaii and from the Florida keys to the Alaskan tundra.

Yet it is not necessary to rely upon metaphysical reasons for urging a return to the balance of powers conceived by the Founding Fathers and written into a supreme law that must be obeyed until the States themselves amend it. There are sound political reasons also. And the foremost of these is that the separate States ought to remain free—as free as possible—to engage in experiment and innovation. I appreciate the argument that this freedom of political action may not promote the most efficient government; it may not be the best for Getting Things Done. But it permits us to avoid the blighting curse of uniformity and regimentation which must always be the foe of creative political thought.

I know of no one who has summed up this position more admirably than Mr. Justice Harlan, in the notable dissenting opinion he wrote in the Roth-Alberts case in 1957. Two men had been convicted for trafficking in obscene materials. Roth under the Federal postal laws, Alberts under the State law of California. A majority of the court voted to uphold both sentences. Harlan objected. He was ready to concur in Alberts' conviction, for this was under State law; and the court's function, in judging the constitutionality of such a statute, was not to decide whether California's policy were wise, or whether the assumptions underlying the State's obscenity law were sound. "Nothing in the Constitution requires California to accept as truth the most advanced and sophisticated psychiatric opinion." The first question was whether the Constitution prohibited California from enacting the law; if not, the Court's only remaining duty was to decide whether Alberts had been denied due process at his trial.

Satisfied that California had the power to enact, and that no reversible error had occurred in the trial itself, Harlan willingly affirmed this judgment. But the companion Roth case was something else. I should like to quote at some length from this dissent, for Harlan's comments, while they necessarily dealt with the narrow and unsavory case before the court, also embraced some of the broad principles that go into the case for States' rights. He said:

> We are faced here with the question whether the Federal obscenity statute, as construed and applied in this case, violates the First Amendment to the Constitution. To me, this question is of quite a different order than one where we are dealing with State legislation under the Fourteenth Amendment. I do not think it follows that State and Federal powers in this area are the same....
>
> The Constitution differentiates between those areas of human conduct subject to the regulation of the States and those subject to the powers of the Federal government. The substantive powers of the two governments, in many instances, are distinct....
>
> The Federal government has, for example, power to restrict seditious speech directed against it, because that Government certainly has the substantive authority to protect itself against revolution. But in dealing with obscenity we are faced with the converse situation, for the interests which obscenity statutes purportedly protect are primarily entrusted to the care, not of the Federal government, but of the States. Congress has no substantive power over sexual morality. Such powers as the Federal government has in this field are but incidental to its other powers, here the postal power, and are not of the same nature as those possessed by the States, which bear direct responsibility for the protection of the local moral fabric....
>
> Not only is the federal interest in protecting the nation against pornography attenuated, but the dangers of federal censorship in this field are far greater than anything the States may do. It has often been said that we have, in the forty-eight States, forty-eight experimental social laboratories.... Different States will have different attitudes toward the same work of literature. The same book which is freely read in one State might be classed as obscene in another. And it seems to me that no overwhelming danger to our freedom to experiment and to gratify our tastes in literature is likely to result from the suppression of a borderline book in one of the States, so long as there is no nationwide suppression of the book, and so long as other States are free to experiment with the same or bolder books.
>
> Quite a different situation is presented, however, where the Federal government imposes the ban. The danger is perhaps not great if the people of one State,

through their legislature, decide that "Lady Chatterley's Lover" goes so far beyond the acceptable standards of candor that it will be deemed offensive and nonsellable, for the State next door is still free to make its own choice. But the dangers to free thought and expression are truly great if the Federal government imposes a blanket ban over the nation on such a book. The prerogative of the States to differ on their ideas of morality will be destroyed, the ability of the States to experiment will be stunted. The fact that the people of one State cannot read some of the works of D. H. Lawrence seems to me, if not wise or desirable, at least acceptable. But that no person in the United States should be allowed to do so seems to me to be intolerable, and violative of both the letter and the spirit of the First Amendment.

It is precisely this intolerable end that lies down the path of centralization in the United States. I have strong reservations about extension of the franchise in Georgia and Kentucky to young men and women of eighteen, for I incline to the view that the franchise should not be broadened, but restricted. Yet I am delighted to see them undertake the experiment. If my prejudice be in error, it may be abandoned in the light of their successful experience: but there would be no way of learning this on a small scale if the Congress, by some distortion of its power to alter State regulations prescribing the manner of holding elections, were to extend the franchise overnight to all eighteen-year-olds everywhere. By the same token, I have been interested to see Nevada experiment with divorce laws that are liberal, and South Carolina adhere to divorce laws that are strict. Much has been learned through the varying approaches of the separate States to problems of forestry, steam pollution, conditions of labor, and public education. In a thousand areas of human conduct, the States and their constituent localities constantly are experimenting, and this political ferment—this bubbling vitality— seems to me absolutely essential to the continued strength of the Republic as a whole.

One of the reasons for the success of this system is that the States and the localities must always be closer to the people than the central government. In stating this view, I respectfully differ from one of my brother essayists, who paints a pretty picture of the intimacy that exists, especially in the case of the farmer, between the Federal government and the individual citizen. It is a pretty picture, but a false one. On my own observations (apart from the common observation of mankind), I would find him clearly wrong. Several years ago, in a manifestation of that particular lunacy to which newspapermen historically are prone, I undertook to run a chicken farm. The county agent was indeed a source of comfort, and the home-demonstration worker could be summoned to educate my wife in the mysteries of a churn. But only in a very narrow and technical sense were these neighborly plenipotentiaries ministers of the Federal government. In their appointment and in their daily activities, they were "country people," different in every way from the regional inspectors of the Commodity Credit Corporation sent out to measure one's acres of wheat. Nor were the ministrations of even the county agents and soil conservation committeemen (locally elected) the be-all and end-all of farm life. Of far greater importance were the local schools, and the local tax rate, and the widening of the road that led to the country store. The government that counted most, because we felt the greatest sense of community with it, was the government at the courthouse, and the government at the State Capitol.

A part of this feeling rests in the belief that local government can be controlled in a way that the central government cannot be controlled. Restraints can be applied close at hand, through the devices of referendum and recall, that cannot be applied far away. The county commissioner dwells low on Olympus, and the local alderman is accessible in ways that United States Senators and Cabinet Secretaries are not accessible. When a citizen of Virginia travels to the Capitol at Richmond, he travels with a sure sense of participation and of community; he speaks to the committees of the General Assembly, supporting or opposing particular legislation, as a fellow-citizen in the community of four million that is Virginia. When he travels to the Capitol at Washington, by contrast, he feels insecurity gnawing at his vitals. He finds the palace ringed by the glassy castles of potent baronies—the Machinists, the Mineworkers, the Educationists—and the marbled catacombs of the Senate Office Building are filled with total strangers. In this distant opulence, he stands subdued.

It is out of this sense of helplessness that the citizen draws his prudent fear of "Federal control." He sees Federal control as as inescapable corollary of "Federal aid." He knows that it cannot possibly be otherwise. Nor is he the least impressed by the remonstrances of political doctors who assure him that the history of numerous grant-in-aid programs fails to support his apprehension.

I am told that Federal controls never have been oppressive, and that Federal outlays almost invariably are administered by State and local functionaries in whom our trust may be freely reposed. I am told that I am conjuring mere spectres and seeing things in the dark. John Marshall long ago (in McCulloch *v.* Maryland, 1819) struck through these specious assurances with a famous line. The tax levied by Maryland upon the Bank of the United States was not large; Mr. McCulloch could have paid it and the Bank would not have gone under. But it was not the particular tax that mattered. It was the power to tax, for "the power to tax involves the power to destroy." And Marshall, agreeing for once with Jefferson, scoffed at the idea of having *confidence* in the States to exercise this power wisely:

> If the States may tax one instrument employed by the government in the execution of its powers, they may tax any and every other instrument. They may tax the mail; they may tax the mint; they may tax patent rights; they may tax the papers of the custom-house; they may tax judicial process; they may tax all the means employed by the government, to an excess which would defeat all the ends of government. This was not intended by the American people. They did not design to make their government dependent upon the States.

The same line of reasoning exactly persuades me to sound a warning against the growing absorption of responsibilities by the central government. It never was intended for the people to be dependent upon Washington, either. If the central government can aid our disabled, and pension our old people, and succour our illegitimate children; if it can fill our fish ponds and level our slums; if it can build our highways and lay our sewers and vaccinate our children and finance our college students, it can dominate our lives in such a way that freedom is lost altogether. It is *the power to control* that is to be feared; and this power to control follows the Federal dollar as surely as that famous lamb accompanied little Mary. And it will follow us to school one day if the principle of general aid to public education, and especially to teacher salaries, ever is approved by the Congress.

Coming events cast long shadows. I see the penumbra approaching and I feel the damp wind cold on my neck. Let the man who imagines there are "no controls" study the disbursement of hospital construction grants under the Hill-Burton Act. Let him gaze upon the thick manual of federally approved regulations by which the interstate highways must be constructed uniformly. Let him ponder the effect of the wage controls decreed under the Davis-Bacon Act—40,000 local determinations a year, and every one of them controlling what shall be paid carpenters, pipefitters, and common laborers. We have lately had the example of what is known euphemistically as the National Defense Education Act, and I find in it incipiently the very philosophy that seems to me so dangerous; for these grants are intended chiefly for students agreeable to studying what the government wants them to study—science, and mathematics, and foreign languages. We have opened our classroom door, like the flap of the nomad's tent, to a very large camel. I see in the history of legislation under the commerce clause what lies ahead in education; for the regulation of commerce that began with the steamboats of Gibbons and Ogden has expanded until even the window washers on a local office building are the objects of Federal control. The scholarship program that begins with a subtle hint of what should be learned will yet end in effective control of what shall be taught, and to whom, and by whom, and in what sort of buildings.

It was to this sort of *immoderate greatness* that Gibbon attributed the decline of Rome. It is to this sort of faceless nationalizing, to these idiot yells for *equality,* that our own Republic may yet succumb. Long ago a petty despot, troubled by insurrection in his realm, sent an envoy to Periander for advice. The Ambracian tyrant did not reply directly. He took the envoy into a cornfield, and with a sharp blade lopped off the tallest ears until all stalks were standing level. The despot's solution, he meant to say, lay in chopping down the strong to equality with the weak, for when all men are equal none can excel.

The hard counsel of Periander is lost upon some of the more

# The Case for "States' Rights"

naïve envoys of today's zealous centralizers, but we may be sure it is not wasted on their masters. Their god is the brutal bulldozer, squat as a pagan idol, whose function is to bring down the mountains and to fill up the valleys. They fear excellence as they abhor ineptitude. The diversity of the States offends their pretty sense of order, and from the comfortable living rooms of Scarsdale they weep tears for Mississippi.

The worst fate that could befall this Republic would be for the centralists to impose upon this broad land a Procrustean uniformity that would impoverish the Hudson Valley to enrich the catfish Yazoo. If our strength be in union, it lies first in apartness. This concept is the spark that kindled the American flame; it is the very soul of our Republic, and we ought never to trade it off to the centralist Mephistopheles who promises a beautiful Utopia but would deliver a dreary Hell.

In thus contending for a tightly limited central government, no thoughtful States' righter would want to be misunderstood. If he urges the importance of the Tenth Amendment, he urges with equal vigor the propriety of Article I, Section 8. In matters of foreign policy, in the waging of war, in the coinage of money, in the full and efficient operation of all those delegated powers that are in fact national in their scope—in all of these, the advocate of strict construction yields to the central authority gladly. He is not asking that Delaware be admitted to NATO, or that a first reliance in some war with Russia be placed on the Georgia militia.

He is urging simply that we cherish a reasoned veneration for established institutions, and that we preserve a decent obedience to the form and spirit and meaning of the Constitution. He knows that fallible man will err, and he conceives it better to risk wrongs imposed upon one State than to hazard misjudgments that fall upon fifty. He is no foe of "national greatness." He is merely convinced that national greatness may best be achieved by building upon the solid foundation of personal liberty, individual attainment, and local responsibility erected by the wisest men the Republic will ever know.

# Harry V. Jaffa

•

# "PARTLY FEDERAL, PARTLY NATIONAL": ON THE POLITICAL THEORY OF THE CIVIL WAR

Sir, I know that the discussion of the elementary principles of government is dry and uninteresting; indeed, all abstract discussion is so ... [but] I think it is greatly to be regretted that the true principles of our free institutions have not been more frequently the subject of discussion. The clear comprehension and maintenance of them is essential to the liberty of the people. To obliterate or obscure them will always be, as it always has been, the purpose of those who would misrule and oppress the people.

—Senator Rowan of Kentucky
*in the Debate on Foot's Resolution,
February 8, 1830.*

In 1964 Governor George Wallace vainly attempted to interpose the authority of the state of Alabama to prevent the enforcement of a federal court order for the enrollment of Negroes in the University of Alabama. With this failure, the doctrine of state rights, founded upon the doctrine of state sovereignty, may have reached its end as an effective force within American politics. Yet the ambiguity in the American regime, in virtue of which these doctrines came to life, remains. Still more, the problem which caused the ambiguity, being itself endemic to modern politics, if not to politics simply, also remains. In attempting to understand the dispute concerning sovereignty—or supremacy—within the American regime, we attempt to understand, at its deepest level, this ambiguity and this problem.

In his message to Congress on July 4, 1861, Abraham Lincoln declared that the people of the South would never have rebelled against the national authority, had they not been first convinced that to do so was in fact not rebellion at all, but the exercise of a lawful right under the Constitution.

> It might seem, at first thought, to be of little difference, [Lincoln wrote] whether the present movement at the South be called "secession" or "rebellion." The movers, however, well understood the difference. At the beginning they knew they could never raise their treason to any respectable magnitude by any name which implies *violation* of law. They knew that their people possessed as much moral sense, as much devotion to law and order, and as much pride in, and reverence for, the history and Government of their common country, as any other civilized and patriotic people.... Accordingly ... they invented an ingenious sophism, which, if conceded, was followed by perfectly logical steps ... to the complete destruction of the Union. The sophism itself is, that any State of the Union may, *consistently* with the national Constitution, and therefore *lawfully* and *peacefully,* withdraw from the Union without the consent of the Union or of any other State....
>
> With rebellion thus sugar-coated they have been drugging the public mind of their section for more than thirty years, and until at length they have brought many good men to a willingness to take up arms against the Government the day *after* some assemblage of men have enacted the farcical pretense of taking their State out of the Union, who could have been brought to no such thing the day before.[1]

We can understand the anguish that impelled Lincoln to speak so harshly of the "movers" of the rebellion, as the crisis of the Union broke upon him. Yet there is little reason to believe that, if there had been deception, the movers were less deceived than the moved. Lincoln's assertion that the public mind of the South had been drugged for more than thirty years is itself a confession of the depth and pervasiveness of that "ingenious sophism." This ill accords with the hypothesis of a conspiracy of the clever bad men misleading simple good ones. Nor does it tell us why such a sophism should originally have been conceded.

[1] Roy P. Basler (ed.), *Collected Works of Abraham Lincoln* (New Brunswick: Rutgers University Press, 1953), IV, p. 432.

# The Political Theory of the Civil War

The time span indicated by Lincoln takes us back to the nullification crisis. This began with the printing by the South Carolina legislature of the "Exposition and Protest" of 1828, which had been secretly drafted by John C. Calhoun, then vice president of the United States. Calhoun followed the example (as he thought) of Thomas Jefferson, who had secretly drafted the Kentucky Resolutions of 1798 when he was the vice president. The precedent is not merely fortuitous. Throughout the five years of intense controversy that followed the South Carolina Exposition, climaxed by the Ordinance of Nullification of November 24, 1832, the nullifiers always based their constitutional arguments squarely upon the doctrines they alleged to have been set forth in the Kentucky and Virginia Resolutions of 1798, and in Madison's Report of 1800, adopted by the Virginia legislature in that year. If the nullifiers' contentions were correct, the "ingenious sophism" had its origin with Jefferson and Madison, rather than with Calhoun and his associates, and it would have been proper to say that the public mind had been drugged, not for thirty, but for sixty years. Obviously, such a view of our history is inconsistent with that of Abraham Lincoln. Yet surprisingly enough, Professor Berns endorses it, not less than Mr. Kilpatrick. We should hasten to add, however, that most modern authorities seem to concur in the view that the Kentucky and Virginia Resolutions did in fact supply the premises, if not the detailed reasoning, from which the doctrines of nullification and secession might properly be drawn. Yet there is one earlier authority who warns us against these later ones. This is no less a personage than James Madison, who was alive and full of vigor throughout the nullification controversy, and who was relentless and indefatigable in his opposition to the South Carolina doctrines. He repeatedly and elaborately denied any validity to the arguments purporting to ground those doctrines upon what he and Jefferson had written and done thirty years before. While historians have generally noted this fact no one has, so far as I know, weighed Madison's contentions—or South Carolina's rebuttals—by the theoretical standards to which they themselves appeal.

In his essay on "What the Framers Meant by Federalism," Professor Diamond points out that federalism, prior to the Constitution of 1787, referred to a "voluntary association of states," for

# Harry V. Jaffa

purposes of common advantage, in which no powers of government properly so called, were surrendered to the association. The term "federal government" would have been a solecism, since to be federal meant by definition to be a league resting ultimately on the good faith of the associates, while to be a government meant to have powers of lawful coercion. The government created by the Constitution, by being "partly federal and partly national," as Madison says in *Federalist* 39, corresponded to no prior theoretical understanding of what either the federal or the national was. It is not surprising that in controversies concerning the nature of the regime, the partisans should choose between its federalism and its nationalism, and interpret the one in the light of the other. In the nullification crisis, South Carolina made a resolute attempt systematically to reduce the national features to the federal. It is our thesis that the Carolinians failed in their attempt; yet we would have to admit an equal doubt that the pure nationalists succeeded better in their opposite attempt. Both sides appeared to concede that, as Calhoun was reputed to have said, sovereignty was like chastity, and that it could not be surrendered in part. To call the Constitution of the United States partly national and partly federal was very much like saying that in the new Union, the states were neither maids nor matrons, but that their status was nevertheless legitimate. Clearly there was a new and imperfectly understood "family" relationship in this Union. The rights of the respective parties were far from settled by the Founding Fathers; and yet, as Lincoln declared in 1861:

> A husband and wife may be divorced, and go out of the presence, and beyond the reach of each other; but the different parts of our country cannot do this. They cannot but remain face to face; and intercourse, either amicable or hostile, must continue between them.[2]

Let us now turn to South Carolina which, in its attempt to annul its relationship with the other states in 1832, addressed these words, among others, to them:

> We hold, then, that, on their separation from the Crown of Great Britain, the several colonies became free and independent States, each enjoying the separate and indepen-

[2] *Ibid.*, p. 269.

dent right of self-government; and that no authority can be exercised over them, or within their limits, but by their consent, respectively given as States.[3]

That is to say, South Carolina believed that in declaring independence of Great Britain, each of the thirteen states was, at the same time, declaring its *de jure* independence of each other. Of course, at the moment of independence the new states were not *de facto* independent of each other, since they were jointly conducting a war against Great Britain, upon the success of which their actual independence was contingent. By this view of the Revolution, the United States was then in much the same political condition as the United Nations in World War II. Moreover, the Articles of Confederation do affirm that "each State retains its sovereignty, freedom, and independence, and every power, jurisdiction, and right, which is not by this Confederation expressly delegated to the United States in Congress assembled." It is of the highest importance to notice that, while "power, jurisdiction, and right" are delegated, "sovereignty, freedom, and independence" are retained. Accordingly, the United States may today submit to the jurisdiction of, let us say, the World Court, without abandoning in the smallest degree its sovereignty or freedom. But the position adopted by South Carolina in 1832, allegedly upon the authority of Jefferson and Madison, maintained that the Constitution did not differ in the decisive respect from the Confederation. While more powers may have been delegated, and while these powers may have been permitted to operate directly upon the citizens of the several states, sovereignty, they said, remained where it had been. As a result, each state retained among its reserved powers the power to prevent the operation of these delegated powers within its borders and upon its citizens. Whether this preventive power was called interposition or nullification, its essence was the power to suspend one or more of the powers it had delegated to the United States in the Constitution. In the Address of the Convention to the people of South Carolina, it was further argued that:

> The constitution of the United States, as is admitted by contemporaneous writers, is a compact between sovereign

[3] Address to the People of the United States, Appendix to Gales & Seaton's *Register,* 22nd Cong., 2nd sess., p. 169.

States. Though the subject-matter of that compact was a Government, the powers of which Government were to operate to a certain extent upon the people of those sovereign States aggregately, and not upon the State authorities, as is usual in confederacies, still the constitution is a confederacy. First. It is a confederacy, because, in its foundations, it possesses not one single feature of nationality. The people of the separate States, as distinct political communities, ratified the Constitution, each State acting for itself, and binding its own citizens, and not those of any other State. The act of ratifying declares it "to be binding on the States so ratifying."[4]

It should be observed that Article VII of the Constitution declares that "the ratification of the conventions of nine States shall be sufficient for the establishment of this Constitution between the States so ratifying." Moreover, James Madison, in *The Federalist,* in examining the question of what the relation would be between the nine or more states ratifying, and those failing to do so, concluded that "no political relation [could] subsist between the assenting and the dissenting States." This would seem to bear out the Carolina contention that the acts of ratification alone made the states members of the Union. It would appear to be in massive contradiction to the position taken by Webster and Jackson in 1832, and by Lincoln in 1861, that the Union was older than and prior to the states, and that the states had no political existence outside the Union.[5] As we shall see, the meaning of the Tenth Amendment

[4] *Ibid.,* p. 163.
[5] "In our colonial state, although dependent on another power, we very early considered ourselves as connected by common interest with each other. Leagues were formed for common defence, and, before the declaration of independence, we were known in our aggregate character as the United Colonies of America. That decisive and important step was taken jointly. We declared ourselves a nation by a joint, not by several acts, and . . . agreed . . . [to] form one nation for the purposes of conducting some certain domestic concerns and all foreign relations." Andrew Jackson, Proclamation, December 10, 1832. (Appendix, Gales & Seaton's *Register,* 22nd Cong., 2nd sess., p. 186.)

"The original [States] passed into the Union even *before* they cast off their British colonial dependence; and the new ones each came into the Union directly from a condition of dependence, excepting Texas. And even Texas, in its temporary independence, was never designated a State." Abraham Lincoln, Message to Congress, July 4, 1861. (Basler, *Collected Works of Abraham Lincoln,* IV, p. 433.)

turns decisively upon the question of whether the states are conceived to have this prior and independent existence. In the speeches and letters of the time, we find it endlessly repeated, as Madison says in a letter of 1833 to Daniel Webster, "that compact, express or implied, is the vital principle of free governments as contradistinguished from governments not free; and that a revolt against this principle leaves no choice but between anarchy and despotism." Now if the states are the communities created by the original social compact, the compact which took their citizens out of the state of nature, and if this compact has never been dissolved or modified in any authoritative manner, then it would appear that the states must have created the Constitution. And while it would be true to say that they have a legal status *in* the Constitution, it would not follow that they have their legal status *from* the Constitution. South Carolina claimed a lawful right, both to nullify federal laws, and to secede. Yet South Carolina did not say that the right to secede was a right granted *by* the Constitution. Rather did it hold that the rights in question were rights which it had reserved, rights which had not been delegated, and which were necessary incidents of the sovereignty which had been vested in the state by the social compact of its citizens.[6] And let us repeat, that it was conceded on all sides that the social compact was the vital principle of free government, and that such compact was the origin both of sovereignty and of political obligation. Thus, the Carolinians continue,

[6] "If we are asked upon what ground we place the right to resist a particular law of Congress, and yet regard ourselves as a constituent member of the Union, we answer, the ground of the compact. [Note this refers to the constitutional compact between the states, not the social compact proper.] We do not choose . . . to recur to what are called our natural rights, or the right of revolution. We claim to nullify by a more imposing title. We claim it as a constitutional right, not meaning, as some have imagined, that we derive the right from the constitution . . . it being distinctly understood, at the time of ratifying the constitution, that the exercise of all sovereign rights, not agreed to be had conjointly, were to be exerted separately by the States. Though it be true that the provision in favor of what we call the reserved rights of the States was not necessary to secure to the States such reserved rights, yet the mere circumstance of its insertion in the instrument makes it as clear a constitutional provision as that of the Congress to raise armies or declare war. Any exercise of a right in conformity with a constitutional provision, we conceive to be a constitutional right, whether it be founded on an express grant of the right, or be included in a general reservation of undefined powers." Appendix to Gales & Seaton's *Register,* 22nd Cong., 2nd sess., p. 165.

## Harry V. Jaffa

> The States are [the] authors [of the Constitution]; their power created it; their voice clothed it with authority; the Government it formed is in reality their Government; and the Union, of which it is the bond, is a Union of States, and not of individuals.[7]

In the same letter to Daniel Webster, Madison distinguished the pure nationalist theory of the Constitution, according to which the Union is a compact of the American people taken as an aggregate of individuals, from that theory which holds that the social compact was made solely at the level of the states. In the former case, he observes, the dissolution of the Union would return every man to the state of nature; in the latter, each individual would still live under the protection of the government of his state. Yet Madison does not hesitate to say that the dissolution of the Union would leave the states intact.

> Secondly. It is a confederacy, because the extent of the powers of the Government depends not upon the people of the United States collectively, but upon the State Legislatures, or on the people of the separate States acting in their State conventions, each State being represented by a single vote.[8]

Here the Carolinians refer to the amending power, which they treat as the ultimate power, not merely of changing, but of expounding the Constitution. The amending power represents the ultimate constituent power of the people of all the states, as it is found within the framework of the Constitution. And this power, they point out, is not exercised by any majority of all the people collectively, as an aggregate of individuals, but by the people of the states, acting through the states, whether by the regular state legislatures or by conventions.

> It must never be forgotten that it is to the creating and to the controlling power that we are to look for the true character of the Federal Government, for the present controversy is not as to the sources from which the ordinary powers of government are drawn: these are partly federal

[7] *Register,* p. 169.
[8] *Ibid.,* p. 169.

116

and partly national. Nor is it relevant to consider upon whom these powers operate. In this last view, the Government, for limited purposes, is entirely national. The true question is, who are the parties to the compact? Who created it, and who can alter and destroy it? ... We repeat that, as regards the foundation and extent of its powers, the Government of the United States is ... a league between several sovereigns. ...[9]

The foregoing clearly echoes Madison's summary view of the Constitution at the end of *Federalist* 39. But where Madison says that the Constitution is "in strictness, neither a national nor a federal Constitution, but a composition of both," the Carolinians say that it must, in strictness, be one or the other. And they say it is federal. The meaning that Professor Diamond says belonged to federalism before the new Constitution was drawn up is still the only meaning recognized by South Carolina in 1832. Their only visible concession to novelty is in their combining the word "federal" with the word "government." To what extent this is a concession undermining the integrity of their entire position remain to be seen.

Professor Berns, in his essay on "The Meaning of the Tenth Amendment," argues that this amendment did nothing to alter the distribution of power already provided, nor did it do more than declare that all the powers not delegated had been reserved—a tautology or, at best, a truism. Yet Mr. Kilpatrick calls the Tenth Amendment "the key that unlocks every mystery of our form of government" and "the polar star of our fundamental charter." But Mr. Kilpatrick only echoes Jefferson who, in his opinion on the constitutionality of the first bank of the United States, had declared that he considered "the foundation of the Constitution as laid on this ground—that all powers not delegated to the United States by the Constitution, nor prohibited by it to the States, are reserved to the States, or to the people." Later, in the Kentucky Resolutions, Jefferson again repeats the language of the Tenth Amendment—three times—in magisterial cadences that recall the opening paragraphs of the Declaration of Independence. It is dif-

[9] *Ibid.*, p. 170.

ficult to reconcile this almost liturgical symbolism with the view of the amendment as a mere truism, eminent as the authorities are who take this view. Yet Jefferson himself, in the Kentucky Resolutions, prefaces each recitation of the amendment by saying that it is "true as a general principle" and yet that it must be "expressly declared." Thus Jefferson anticipates the South Carolina Convention's assertion that, on the one hand, the amendment was not needed to establish the reserved powers of the states, and yet that by doing so, it made such powers "express," and therefore as unquestionable as the expressly enumerated powers. The Kentucky Resolutions seem to have planted in the political consciousness of the nation—or of a large part of it—the proposition that the Constitution *expressly* declares that all powers not delegated have been reserved. This in turn has led some commentators to read the amendment *as if* it had said that all powers not *expressly* delegated had been reserved.

Yet there is an ambiguity concerning "the people" both in the Preamble and in the Tenth Amendment which lends a certain plausibility if not authority to such an error. We must recall that by the social compact theory *all* the "just powers" of government are delegated, those of the states no less than those of the United States. There are, in the Tenth Amendment, two reservations of powers: the first is "to the States respectively," and the second is "to the people." Thus the people have delegated some governmental powers to the United States, and some to the states, and those they have delegated to neither they have retained. But who are the people? This question is difficult to answer because the word itself may take the same form whether in the singular or the plural. If the "people" of the United States are conceived as united by the social compact only on the level of the individual states, then it is the combined "peoples" of the different states to whom we are referring. But then the Tenth Amendment should have read that the powers not delegated are reserved "to the States, or to the people of the States respectively." Such a reading of the Tenth Amendment is, we maintain, plausible. And we should observe that it is no less a truism than that of Chief Justice Marshall or Justice Story—but it is an entirely different truism. And it is this truism which appears to be favored by Jefferson in the Kentucky Resolutions, when he wrote that the several states had constituted "a general government for special purposes . . . reserving each State to itself, the residuary mass of right to their own self-government." The phrase "each State . . . itself" seems to imply that sovereignty is reserved "to the people of each state."

The tension between the two alternative conceptions of the people of the United States may be seen by a backward look at the struggle over ratification of the Constitution. The opponents, known paradoxically as the anti-Federalists, had charged that the Constitution was designed to destroy the states, and to establish one "consolidated" government. For example, Robert Yates of New York, under the pseudonym of "Brutus," had declared in 1788 that

> . . . this Constitution, if it is ratified, will not be a compact entered into by the States, in their corporate capacities, but an agreement of the people of the United States, as one great body politic. . . .

And again:

> The first object declared to be in view is, "To form a perfect union." It is to be observed, it is not an union of states of bodies corporate; had this been the case the existence of the state governments, might have been secured. But it is a union of the people of the United States considered as one body, who are to ratify this constitution, if it is adopted.[10]

Thus Yates in 1788 gives the Constitution an interpretation exactly opposite to that given it by the South Carolina Convention in 1832. Of course, in the debate over ratification it was the interest of the opponents of the Constitution thus to characterize it, just as it was the interest of the advocates to deny this characterization. After ratification, these positions were in a certain sense reversed. Yet it was James Madison, as the leading nationalist in the Constitutional Convention, and the leading advocate of ratification in Virginia, who took the initiative in the First Congress to produce in the Bill of Rights such a statement as finally appeared as the Tenth Amend-

[10] Cecilia Kenyon (ed.), *The Antifederalists* (Indianapolis: Bobbs-Merrill, 1966), p. 345.

ment. He did so largely to persuade the anti-Federalists that such fears as those expressed by Yates were unfounded, and that the delegated powers of the general government would not swallow up the functions of the governments of the states.

It is of some interest to observe an error that Yates appears to make in giving the language of the Preamble. He cites its purpose "to form a perfect Union." Yet in the logic of the social compact theory, a "perfect union" differed from a "more perfect union" as much as "powers not delegated" differed from "powers not expressly delegated." Men in a state of nature, agreeing to form that union which is the body politic or civil society, do these two things. First they agree unanimously to have such a body politic. This unanimity is necessary, because whoever does not agree is no part of the body; and whoever does agree, is henceforward part of the body, and bound by its decisions. Secondly, in agreeing to be part of the body politic, each consents that the exercise of the executive power of the law of nature—the right to be judge in his own cause—is entirely surrendered. It is this unanimous consent, and the concomitant surrender of the executive power of the law of nature, which is the vital principle of free society. It is this which makes civil society a voluntary association which yet may lawfully coerce. It is this which makes every civil society proper a "perfect union."

We see then that Yates's error was necessary to his thesis: namely, that the Constitution abolished the social compact, in virtue of which the states possessed the sovereignty which was reserved to them in the Articles of Confederation. At the same time, we must observe it *is* an error. A "more perfect union" can only be one in which a perfecting process is applied to a preexisting union. And that preexisting union was assuredly one, not of individuals, but of states. The ambiguity, the mystery, of the Tenth Amendment, and of the reserved powers of "the people," remains.

To the South Carolina Convention of 1832, the rights of nullification and secession were necessary to secure the right of the people to be governed only by those just powers to which they had consented, a right which had been solemnly declared on July 4, 1776. They were *lawful* as distinct from *revolutionary* safeguards, because they could be asserted by the people of the state, acting in accordance with the same peaceful and lawful procedures by which the state had ratified the Constitution. Yet the Carolinians were faced with their own admission that "the subject-matter of that compact [viz., the Constitution] was a Government." And if that government was the mere agent of sovereign states, with no inherent powers of its own, it was nonetheless the agent of *all* the states. An unqualified unilateral veto by one state upon a governmental action not only contradicted the idea inherent in government, it contradicted the right of sovereign states to even form a league with such an agent as South Carolina proclaimed the government of the United States to be. Under the guidance of John C. Calhoun, South Carolina adopted the theory of the concurrent majority, which was an attempt to strike some kind of a balance between the idea of a mere league and that of a national government representing "one people." When a sovereign state nullified an act of the general government, said to be the exercise of a power not delegated, it was not in fact absolute and unconditional. It was a suspensory rather than a final veto. If a constitutional convention were to propose delegating the power in question, and if such proposal were to be adopted as an amendment by three-fourths of the states, by any of the procedures described in Article V of the Constitution, South Carolina would recede from its position. Or, rather, it would accept the power as being now authorized by the sovereign powers of the states.[11]

Yet this led to a difficulty hardly less than that for which it offered a solution. The Constitution had been adopted by *all* the states. And the South Carolina Convention had declared that this unanimous consent, and the provision in the Constitution that it was to be established only "between the States so ratifying" it, was evidence that sovereignty remained in the states. It was the seventh article of the original Constitution, more than anything else in that document, which justified, in their own eyes, their assertion that the Tenth Amendment was not strictly necessary for securing the reserved rights of the states. Yet amendments might be made by three-fourths of the states. By what right might *three-fourths* now

[11] *Register,* p. 167.

do what hitherto could rightfully be done only by *all?* In the state of nature, all must consent to form civil society; but from this unanimous consent arises the sovereign authority of the *majority.* The only way in which the social compact might authorize government other than that of the majority, is by delegation from the sovereign majority. We may observe the difficulty faced by South Carolina in maintaining the idea of state sovereignty, in the presence of the idea of the concurrent majority, in the following passage from Calhoun's draft of the South Carolina Exposition of 1828. This is the composition which contains the seminal ideas informing the work of the South Carolina Convention of 1832. The emphasis has been supplied to two crucial passages.

> ... by an express provision of the Constitution, it may be amended by three-fourths of the States; and thus each State, by assenting to the Constitution with this provision, *has modified its original right as a sovereign,* of making its individual consent necessary to any change in its political condition; and, by becoming a member of the Union, has placed this important power in the hands of three-fourths of the States—*in whom the highest power known to the Constitution actually resides.*

Professor Freehling has pointed out that the South Carolina legislature changed Calhoun's draft, so that in the published version "has modified its original right as a sovereign" became "has surrendered its original right as a sovereign," and "in whom the highest power known to the Constitution actually resides" became "in which the sovereignty of the Union ... does now actually reside."[12]

Now if sovereignty is indivisible, as the Convention of 1832 also declared (in accordance with what Calhoun had elsewhere maintained), then Calhoun's "modified" sovereignty had to become the "surrendered" sovereignty of the South Carolina legislature. Yet by the logic of the same theory, in virtue of which sovereignty is indivisible, it could not be given up to three-fourths of the states. If sovereignty had been surrendered, it must have been surrendered to the one people of the entire United States, who, by the consent—

---

[12] William W. Freehling, *Prelude to Civil War: The Nullification Controversy in South Carolina, 1816–1836.* (New York: Harper and Row, 1965), pp. 167, 168.

implicit or express—of the numerical majority, might have authorized the three-fourths of the states to exercise the amending power.

But if sovereignty had been surrendered to the Union, then the sovereign power of the Union might be exercised "in all cases whatsoever." That is to say, three-fourths of the states, exercising the sovereignty residing in the majority of the people of the United States and embracing all their "reserved powers," might do anything which "to them shall seem most likely to effect their Safety and Happiness." A sovereign is by definition a source and not a subject of law. Yet we find it stipulated in Article V, as part of the amending power itself, "that no State, without its Consent, shall be deprived of its equal suffrage in the Senate." Given this stipulation, equal force would seem to attach as well to the provision, in Article IV, that no new states might be formed by the junction of two or more states, without the consent of the states involved, as well as of the Congress. This of course would be necessary to prevent subdivisions or mergers from circumventing the guarantee of equal representation. There are many other features of the Constitution which might profitably be examined to see whether, either independently or as inferences from the ones just mentioned, they might be considered unamendable. Such would certainly include the declaration that "no religious test shall *ever* be required" as a qualification for office under the United States (emphasis supplied) ; as well as the guarantee by the United States to every state of "a Republican Form of Government." One might ask, of course, whether the concept of unamendable provisions could stand in the face of a determination by three-fourths of the states to abolish them. But would it not violate every sense of constitutional propriety to amend the amending procedure itself, by anything less than unanimous consent? To suggest that an amendment might abolish the states is only to say that revolutionary changes might take place under the forms of the Constitution. But the Constitution as originally ratified and subsequently amended seems to have pledged, even against the constituent power of the people, to maintain the states in their prescribed constitutional role, as indestructible components of the Union. However flexibly this role might be interpreted, there would appear to be a design in the Constitution destined forever to prevent the people of the United States from becoming a mere numerical aggregate. It would prevent that people ever from becoming a mere number of individuals as distinct from an organic composite of individuals in states. We would consider then that Vice-President Calhoun in 1828 was wiser than his revisers. He may indeed have been wiser than he himself was elsewhere, when he insisted upon the indivisibility of sovereignty. But he was not wiser than James Madison, the Father of the Constitution, who had seen since 1787 that the new government although a composite of the federal and the national, was yet not reducible to either of these elements. The compact theory of the Constitution, as first set forth in the Kentucky and Virginia Resolutions, and appealed to so confidently by the nullifiers of 1832, did *not,* according to Madison, provide any authority for the concept of individual or separate state sovereignty.

In the following passage from his Proclamation against the nullifiers, President Jackson indicates something of the agreement as well as the difference between the positions then in conflict.

> It is true that the Governor of the State speaks of the submission of their grievances to a convention of all the States, which, he says, they "sincerely and anxiously seek and desire." Yet this obvious and constitutional mode of obtaining the sense of the other States on the construction of the federal compact, and amending it, if necessary, has never been attempted by those who have urged the State on to this destructive measure.[13]

Thus Jackson and the nullifiers *agreed* that a convention of all the states represented an authoritative mode of determining controverted points of constitutional construction. They *differed* concerning the lawfulness of nullification as a device to compel the states to deliver their judgment in this mode. Yet in their agreement lay a recognition *both* of state sovereignty *and* of national supremacy. Neither side could escape from the implications of the other's position, because it was always, in some sense, an element of their own. Jackson had imbibed, according to his own understanding, the doctrine of the Virginia and Kentucky Resolutions; and it is well to remember

[13] *Appendix,* p. 185.

that he combined an ardent strict constructionism with the most thoroughgoing nationalism. Although Lincoln's career as a party politician prior to the repeal of the Missouri Compromise had been that of a Whig, it was the precedent established by Jackson, both of word and of deed, that he followed most closely in the secession crisis. And both Jackson and Lincoln were supported by Madison in their denial that any ground whatever was to be found for that "ingenious sophism" that led logically, both in 1832 and 1861, to the destruction of the Union.

We have already seen that the idea of the concurrent majority implied a decisive modification of the idea of state sovereignty from its original purity. Nullification was, in fact, claimed as an inference from the sovereign right of three-fourths of the states to amend the Constitution, a right which itself was, at best, a kind of quasi-sovereignty. And secession, far from being the direct manifestation of unqualified state sovereignty, was itself a sanction for nullification, and therefore an inference from this inference. Every attempt by the Carolinians, whether in 1832 or 1860, to present the right of secession as a constitutional right, standing squarely on its own feet rather than an indirect consequence of other rights, was hopelessly entangled in self-contradiction.

On the other hand, however, Jackson's reference to the Constitution as "our social compact," if it were taken in the usual sense which implies sovereignty in a numerical majority of the American people, would equally lend itself to self-contradiction. As Madison was to point out to Edward Everett, in the letter that was published in the *North American Review* in 1832,[14] the government of the United States required the active cooperation of the state governments, in the election or selection of all its branches, while the general government plays no role whatever in the selection of the state governments. Moreover, the states have a crucial role, by means of the federal Congress, in the impeachment, and the trial for impeachment, of the federal executive and judiciary, while the general government has no role in the removal of state officers. As long as the constitutional existence of the states is guaranteed, a considerable measure of state sovereignty necessarily accompanies it. Yet Madison

[14] Gaillard Hunt (ed.), *The Writings of James Madison* (New York: Putnam, 1910), IX, pp. 383–403.

denied, in 1830 and thereafter, that such sovereignty ever implied the right of a *single* state to nullify the action of the government of the United States, unless reversed by the action of three-fourths of the states.

Madison was confronted, throughout the nullification crisis, with the language which he had used in 1798 and 1800, and which had been widely if erroneously regarded as supplying justification both for nullification and secession. Let us examine some of that language, and its bearing upon the controversy. The compact theory of the Constitution, which has been held to contain the essence of the doctrine of state sovereignty, appears in the Virginia Resolutions of 1798 as follows:

> That this Assembly doth explicitly and peremptorily declare that it views the powers of the Federal Government as resulting from the compact to which the states are parties, as limited by the plain sense and intention of the instrument constituting that compact; as no further valid than they are authorized by the grants enumerated in that compact, the states, who are parties thereto, have the right and are in duty bound to interpose for arresting the progress of the evil, and for maintaining within their respective limits the authorities, rights, and liberties appertaining to them.

In order to judge fairly what Madison meant by saying that the *states* were the parties to the federal compact, note the ambiguities of the word "state" in the Report of 1800.

> It is indeed true that the term "States" is sometimes used in a vague sense, and sometimes in different senses. . . . Thus it sometimes means the separate sections of territory occupied by the political societies within each; sometimes the particular governments established by those societies; sometimes those societies as organized into those particular governments; and, lastly, it means the people composing those political societies in their highest sovereign capacity.[15]

It is only in this *last* of the four enumerated senses that the word state has been used in the Virginia Resolutions. And as Madison then and thereafter argued, the *states* in their highest sovereign

[15] *Ibid.,* vol. VI, p. 348.

capacity are identical with the *people of the United States* in their highest sovereign capacity. For this people has no political existence, except as people of the respective states.

Madison argued in 1830 and thereafter that the Virginia Resolutions, in calling upon "the states ... to interpose," had reference only to the states collectively. But that the states in their sovereign capacity constitute the highest tribunal known to the Constitution is at least as much a truism as the proposition that all powers not delegated are reserved. Some difficulty may, however, attach to the use here of the word "tribunal." It may be objected that the states in their sovereign capacity do not constitute a tribunal, a term which ought to be reserved for such a body as the Supreme Court. Yet any doubts we might have on this point are resolved by Abraham Lincoln when, in his first inaugural address, he pronounced these magisterial lines:

> Why should there not be a patient confidence in the ulti-
> mate justice of the people? Is there any better, or equal
> hope, in the world? In our present differences, is either
> party without faith of being in the right? If the Almighty
> Ruler of nations, with his eternal truth and justice, be on
> your side of the North, or on yours of the South, that truth,
> and that justice, will surely prevail, by the judgment of
> this great tribunal, the American people.[16]

That the "American people" is the highest of all tribunals known to the Constitution, was then Lincoln's conviction no less than Madison's, notwithstanding the fact that Madison referred to this people, in its highest sovereign capacity, as "the states." It should be also borne in mind that Lincoln, no less than Madison in 1800, rejected the thesis that the Supreme Court was the tribunal in which questions of conflicting jurisdictions should have their final resolution. Madison put it thus in his Report:

> However true, therefore, it may be that the judicial de-
> partment is, in all questions submitted to it by the forms
> of the Constitution, to decide in the last resort, this resort
> must necessarily be deemed the last in relation to the au-
> thorities of the other department of the Government; not in

[16] Basler, IV. p. 270.

relation to the rights of the parties to the constitutional compact, from which the judicial as well as the other departments hold their delegated trusts. On any other hypothesis, the delegation of judicial power would annul the authority delegating it; and the concurrence of this department with the others in usurped powers might subvert forever, and beyond the possible reach of any rightful remedy, the very Constitution which all were instituted to preserve.[17]

This denial of the political, as distinct from the legal supremacy of the Court, was later expressed by Lincoln thus:

I do not forget the position assumed by some, that constitutional questions are to be decided by the Supreme Court; nor do I deny that such decisions must be binding in any case.... At the same time the candid citizen must confess that if the policy of the government, upon vital questions, affecting the whole people, is to be irrevocably fixed by decisions of the Supreme Court, the instant they are made, in ordinary litigation between parties, in personal actions, the people will have ceased, to be their own rulers, having, to that extent, practically resigned their government, into the hands of that eminent tribunal.[18]

We must recall here that, in 1861, it was the seceding states of the South that had demanded that the opinion of the Supreme Court, delivered by Chief Justice Taney in the case of Dred Scott, be accepted as a final judgment as to the true meaning of the Constitution, and binding as such upon the states and upon the people. In their view, the states that had cast their votes for Abraham Lincoln in 1860 had by this fact manifested a determination not to be bound by the Constitution. For Lincoln had been elected upon a platform pledged to the federal prohibition of slavery in the territories, after the Court had declared that legislation to this end was unconstitutional.

Madison, Jackson, and Lincoln all held to the position that the primary remedy for real or alleged usurpations by governments, whether state or federal, was in changing the officers of those governments by free elections. Although the principal charge made against

[17] Hunt, VI, p. 352.
[18] Basler, IV, p. 268.

the Sedition Act, especially in Madison's Report, was that it undermined the integrity of the electoral process, yet in the end Madison declared that the Resolutions were "expressions of opinion, unaccompanied with any other effect than what they may produce on opinion by exciting reflection." He contrasted them with the "expositions of the judiciary" which "are carried into immediate effect by force." If the "interposition" referred to in the Resolutions could not be carried into effect by any legal compulsion, then they could have had nothing in common with the nullification declared by South Carolina in 1832. The purpose of the Virginia Resolutions was to excite those reflections that might result either in the political defeat of the authors of the offending acts, or in amendments to the Constitution. We may note that Lincoln, in 1861, besides defending the sovereign right of the people, by the electoral process, to overrule the Supreme Court's opinions, also endorsed the idea of a constitutional amendment—or amendments —to clarify points of disputed construction. And he preferred, he said, the convention mode,

> in that it allows amendments to originate with the people themselves, instead of only permitting them to take or reject propositions originated by others, not especially chosen for the purpose....[19]

We would particularly call attention to the expression "the people themselves" in a context unmistakably similar to, if not identical with, that in which Madison elsewhere refers to the states in their sovereign capacity.

Throughout American history—at least since July 4, 1776—it has been conceded that all people everywhere have the right to resist intolerable oppression. This is a right which belongs not only to the people of a state, but of any part of a state. Indeed, it belongs to each individual, although it is a right which is seldom valuable to individuals, since they seldom have the power to make resistance effective. But this right—the right of revolution—is a right paramount to the Constitution and to all positive laws whatever. It is a natural right. In his inaugural address Lincoln said that

[19] *Ibid.,* p. 270.

> If, by the mere force of numbers, a majority should deprive
> a minority of any clearly written constitutional right, it
> might, in a moral point of view, justify revolution—cer-
> tainly would, if such a right were a vital one.[20]

As James Madison put it in a paper he wrote on sovereignty,[21] a
majority may do anything that could *rightfully* be done by the
unanimous concurrence of all the members of a civil society. The
rule of the majority being a substitute for unanimity, although itself arising from unanimity, requires that it be exercised only for
ends to which all have consented. Clearly, the degradation of the
minority cannot be one of those ends. Majority rule itself then
cannot be understood as the rule of mere numbers; it must be the
rule of numbers for certain ends. And numbers must then be assembled in a certain way, if they are to be presumed restrained by
the ends for which majority rule was instituted. It was then not
simply a majority whose rule Lincoln endorsed in 1861, but one

> held in restraint by constitutional checks and limitations,
> and always changing easily, with deliberate changes of
> popular opinions and sentiments....[22]

Such a majority is "the only sovereign of a free people." State
rights, as one of the devices to qualify the "mere force of numbers,"
were, to Lincoln no less than to Madison, an essential feature of
that constitutional majority which made the voice of the American
people in some sense the voice of God.

The Kentucky Resolutions differ from those of Virginia in an
important respect, from which many consequences have followed.
Much of the confusion is due to the difference in their meanings.
While Madison took great pains in the great Report of 1800 to
clarify Virginia's resolves of 1798, prudence forbade that he comment openly upon the differences that we know he perceived between the resolutions he had drawn and those that Jefferson had

---

[20] *Ibid.,* p. 267.
[21] Hunt, IX, p. 570.
[22] Basler, IV, p. 268.

secretly drawn for Kentucky. Since the Kentucky Resolutions were published first (November 16, 1798), there has been a tendency then and since to read Virginia's (December 24, 1798) as if they expressed identical views. According to the resolutions drawn by Madison, the Constitution is a compact "to which the States are parties." That is, the states have entered a compact analogous to that entered into by individuals in a state of nature. As the subject of the agreement is a *government,* the states are bound by the *lex majoris partis,* as the *pars major* is defined in the instrument.[23] If the government established by the states—that is, by the people of the states in their highest sovereign capacity—usurps powers not delegated to it, then recourse to the sovereign is possible under the Constitution by any of the modes prescribed therein. But any attempt by one state, or even the people of one state in their highest sovereign capacity, to decide for all, is itself an act of usurpation. As Madison pointed out, over and over again, by adopting the Constitution of the United States, the people of each state formed part of a single nation, as they formed part of a single government, for the purposes specified—or enumerated—in the compact uniting them. The very equality of rights of the states, both as contracting parties whose unanimous consent was required to bring the Constitution into operation, and whose continuous cooperation was necessary to keep the government in operation under the Constitution, made it inadmissible either that one or one-fourth plus one decided for all. The doctrine of the concurrent majority, Madison noted, reverses the logic of the amending clause. Instead of three-fourths deciding for all, one-fourth plus one finally decides, *after* one has completely arrested the motion of the government. But no free government can recognize the permanent rule of the minority. And the right of secession, Madison noted long before Lincoln, leads to the destruction of the rights, not only of the majority, but of the minority as well. He wrote in 1833,

> An inference from the doctrine that a single state has the right to secede at will from the rest is that the rest would have an equal right to secede from it; in other words, to

[23] Cf. Hunt, IX, p. 570.

turn it, against its will, out of its union with them. Such a doctrine would not, till of late, have been palatable any-where, and nowhere less so than where it is now most con-tended for.[24]

These words have a powerful echo in Lincoln's message to Congress of July 4, 1861.

> If all the States, save one, should assert the power to *drive* that one out of the Union, it is presumed that the whole class of seceder politicians would at once deny the power, and denounce the act as the greatest outrage upon State rights. But suppose that precisely the same act, instead of being called "driving the one out," should be called "the seceding of the others from that one," it would be exactly what the seceders claim to do.[25]

In the Kentucky Resolutions, the role of an individual state, as a member of the Union, is presented differently. As in the Virginia Resolutions, the Constitution is a compact, but it is a compact to which

> each State acceded as a State, and is an integral party, its co-States forming, as to itself, the other party. . . .

Whereas Madison conceived each state, by adopting the Constitu-tion, to place itself under the rule of the majority—as majority rule was defined in the Constitution—Jefferson conceived of each state as one of two parties, the other states collectively forming the other party. And of course, where there are only two parties, majority rule is impossible. In fact, the parties remain, in the decisive sense, in the state of nature. As Jefferson puts it,

> . . . the government created by this compact was not made the exclusive or final judge of the extent of the powers dele-gated to itself; since that would have made its discretion, and not the Constitution, the measure of its powers. . . .[26]

[24] *Ibid.,* p. 497.
[25] Basler, IV, p. 436.
[26] Henry S. Commager (ed.), *Documents of American History* (New York: Appleton, 1963), I, p. 178.

Jefferson here lays a foundation for South Carolina's errors, by calling the creation of the compact a "government," while leaving the "final judge" of its powers in a state of nature, as he does when he declares

> ...that as in all other cases of compact among parties having no common Judge, *each party has an equal right to judge for itself, as well of infractions as of the mode and measure of redress.*[27]

There is a relationship of ideas here which is not easy to reconcile within a framework of consistency. Jefferson conceives of a relationship between states and government, which is that of principal and agent. But there can be no adversary relationship between principal and agent, since there is no equality, such as is presupposed in an adversary relationship. The only adversary relationship conceivable is between the individual state and its "co-states." Yet the co-states are presented by Jefferson, not as adversaries, but as partners necessarily having the same interest in retaining all powers not delegated to their common agent. In the ninth resolution, Jefferson has Kentucky declare that

> this commonwealth is determined, as it doubts not its co-States are, tamely to submit to undelegated and consequently unlimited powers in no man or body of men on earth...[28]

Now, of course, the very idea of government based upon the consent of the governed at once excludes the idea of submission to powers not delegated—that is, not consented to—and to the idea of having "no common judge." Jefferson seems to believe that while the states have created a government for certain enumerated purposes, that in all "cases not made federal" the states remain in a state of nature. In these cases not made federal, the same ninth resolution declares that the states have a "natural right" to declare the acts of their common government "void and of no force." But neither in the resolutions of 1798 or those of 1799, which employed

---

[27] *Ibid.*, p. 179.
[28] *Ibid.*

the fatal word "nullification," did Kentucky unequivocally assert a right to *act* upon its declaration. The 1798 resolutions arrive finally at what must have been a lame conclusion to the nullifiers, for they ask at the end only that the co-states "unite with this Commonwealth in requesting . . . the repeal at the next session of Congress" of the offending acts. While those of 1799, even while asserting nullification—which is nowhere defined—as a "rightful remedy," continue by declaring that Kentucky will nonetheless "bow to the laws of the Union."

The mystery of Jefferson's doctrine in the Kentucky Resolutions may perhaps be rendered somewhat less obscure, by a reference provided by Madison in one of his letters, written in 1832. In this letter Madison is emphatic upon the point to which we have already referred, namely, that "In the Virginia Resolutions and Report, the *plural* number, *States,* is in *every* instance used where reference is made to the authority which presided over the Government." The Kentucky Resolutions, however, "being less guarded have been more easily perverted." But, Madison remarks,

> It is remarkable how closely the nullifiers who make the name of Mr. Jefferson the pedestal for their colossal heresy, shut their eyes and lips, whenever his authority is ever so clearly and emphatically against them. You have noticed what he says in his letters to Monroe and Carrington. . . .[29]

We give the references in Jefferson's own words, instead of Madison's summary. To Carrington, Jefferson wrote from Paris, in 1787, in defense of the Articles of Confederation:

> But with all the imperfections of our present government, it is, without comparison, the best existing, or that ever did exist . . . It has so often been said, as to be generally believed, that Congress has no power by the Confederation, to enforce anything; for example, contributions of money. It was not necessary to give them that power expressly; they have it by a law of nature. When two parties make a compact, there results to each a power of compelling the other to execute it. Compulsion was never so easy as in our case, where a single frigate would soon levy

[29] Hunt, IX, p. 491.

on the commerce of any State the deficiency of its con-
tributions....[30]

Earlier, Jefferson had written to Monroe in a similar vein.

> The States must see the rod; perhaps it must be felt by
> some one of them.... Every rational citizen must wish to
> see an effective instrument of coercion....[31]

A fair conclusion from these letters—certainly the one drawn by
Madison—is that Jefferson, while seeing both the Constitution and
the earlier confederation as a compact in which there were but two
parties, saw also a right of compulsion of the weaker by the stronger
party, a right which it possessed by the law of nature. The natural
right referred to in the Kentucky Resolutions becomes then a *re-
minder* to the co-states of their common interest in keeping the
common government within the boundaries of its delegated powers,
and of preserving the states in the possession of all their reserved
powers. Yet if the co-states refuse to concur with the protesting
state, that the common government has usurped powers not delegated, the protesting state has no further recourse except revolution.
And if it chooses to exercise this ultimate right, the co-states assuredly have an equal right under the law of nature to coerce it.
The differences between Jefferson and Madison in 1798 are at
bottom the same as their differences in 1787. Jefferson saw the law
of nature giving powers to the Congress of the Confederation by
implication, which made the revision or replacement of the Articles
less urgent—to put it mildly—than Madison believed it to be. The
appeal to the law of nature, as an element in the continuous implementation of the law of the Constitution, was a constant feature
of Jefferson's thought. The difference between the Virginia and
Kentucky Resolutions can, perhaps, be best seen by considering
Madison's critique of Jefferson's 1783 draft of a constitution for
Virginia, as Madison described it in *Federalist* 49. It would take
us beyond our present purpose to consider this here, except to note

[30] Thomas Jefferson Randolph (ed.), *Correspondence of Thomas Jefferson* (Boston: 1830), II, p. 203.
[31] *Ibid.*, p. 43.

that Madison thought the constant appeal to the natural rights of the people dangerous to the stability of civil society. Yet there can be no doubt that Jackson and Lincoln had as much sanction for using force against South Carolina in 1833 and in 1861 from the Jeffersonian as from the Madisonian standpoint.

It was Jefferson, not Madison, who had recourse to the law of nature, as a power necessarily implied—even if not expressly mentioned—in constitutions. Nevertheless, Madison had no less keen an appreciation than Jefferson of the importance of the law of nature in the foundation of constitutions and of governments. It is instructive therefore to consider once more that section of the Constitution to which South Carolina appealed as the most incontrovertible evidence of state sovereignty. We refer of course, to Article VII, which declares that it requires the ratifications of nine states "for the establishment of this Constitution between the States so ratifying the same." It is a Constitution between *states,* not between *individuals,* and the states have not expressly divested themselves of their sovereignty, so that their sovereignty must remain among their reserved powers—thus ran the most fundamental of all South Carolina's theses. How did James Madison regard this evidence in 1787? We have already noted that he agreed with South Carolina, to the extent that he conceded that "no political relation" could "subsist between the assenting and dissenting States." Yet, he continued in *Federalist* 43, "The claims of justice, both on one side and on the other, will be in force, and must be fulfilled." How the claims of justice are to be regarded in this context, Madison had suggested earlier in the same number, by referring "to the great principle of self-preservation . . . to the transcendent law of nature and of nature's God. . . ." More explicit information on the practical conclusions to be drawn from the existence of a transcendent law of nature must be referred to the whole body of argument in *The Federalist* concerning, not merely the utility, but the absolute necessity of a firm Union to the safety no less than the happiness of the United States. While it was true that during the interval between the time that the new government went into operation and the time the Constitution was ratified by Rhode Island and North Carolina, the latter were, in a certain sense, foreign states. This was more a formal than a substantive truth, for Rhode Island and North

Carolina could never have acted upon their hypothetical independence. The question of what would have happened to them if they had not ratified the Constitution is, in fact, identical with the question of what would have happened had they attempted to form alliances with European powers. Three times, in *Federalist* 43, Madison refers to this question as a "delicate" one, of which "the flattering prospect of its being merely hypothetical forbids an over-curious discussion." When the question ceased to be hypothetical in 1861, Lincoln only followed the dictates of Madison and of Jackson when he declared, "I hold, that in contemplation of universal law, and of the Constitution, the Union of these states is perpetual." And that law, a law at once that of the Constitution and of nature, a law upon which the safety and happiness of the entire United States depended, was enforced.

WALTER BERNS

•

# THE MEANING OF THE
# TENTH AMENDMENT

The powers not delegated to the United States by the Constitution, nor prohibited by it to the States, are reserved to the States respectively, or to the people.

## I

No aspect of the United States Constitution has been so vigorously and so persistently disputed as its division of powers between the national government and the governments of the several states. Whatever may be said of the intent of the men who controlled the 1787 convention and, thereby, may be said to have authored the constitutional document, there can be scarcely any doubt of the intent of the men who provided the principal opposition to its ratification. They spoke in opposition out of a concern for the integrity and authority of the states. They formulated, in the several state ratifying conventions, the original drafts of the first ten amendments to the Constitution which were debated and formally proposed by the First Congress, and they, and their heirs, have resisted the exercise of national authority down to the present day. Fear of national power is a theme running the entire course of our history.

This fear cannot be dismissed as unreasonable. The authors of *The Federalist* might seek to discount it by arguing that the more likely danger was state usurpation of national authority, but their arguments, whatever their effect on the issue then at stake—the ratification of the new Constitution—are not convincing to us who read them with the advantage of a knowledge of subsequent events. "Several important considerations have been touched in the course of these papers," wrote Madison in *Federalist* 45, "which discountenance the supposition that the operation of the federal government will by degrees prove fatal to the state governments. The more I revolve the subject, the more fully I am persuaded that the balance is much more likely to be disturbed by the preponderancy of the last than of the first scale."[1] Yet within a decade he was to join Jefferson in denouncing federal power in the name of state sovereignty. Hamilton, too, argued that it "will always be far more easy for the state governments to encroach upon the national authorities than for the national government to encroach upon the state authorities [because, just as] a man is more attached to his family than to his neighborhood, to his neighborhood than to the community at large, the people of each state would be apt to feel a stronger bias towards their local governments than towards the government of the Union," unless, he warned, "the force of that principle should be destroyed by a much better administration of the latter"[2]—which he promptly set out to provide.

In 1788, Madison and Hamilton might wonder, or at least pretend to wonder, why the proposed Constitution should engender such alarm among the friends of state authority. "If the new Constitution be examined with accuracy and candor," Madison asserted disarmingly, "it will be found that the change which it proposes consists much less in the addition of NEW POWERS to the Union than in the invigoration of its ORIGINAL POWERS [i.e., under the Articles of Confederation]. The regulation of commerce, it is true, is a new power; but that seems to be an addition which few oppose and from which no apprehensions are entertained."[3] And why should there be apprehensions when, according to Hamilton, "the supervision of agriculture and of other concerns of a similar nature, all those things, in short, which are proper to be provided for by local legislation, can never be desirable cares of a general jurisdiction."[4] Yet in 1942 the Supreme Court was to uphold as a valid exercise of the commerce power an Act of Congress making

[1] *The Federalist Papers,* ed. Clinton Rossiter (New York: New American Library, 1961).
[2] *The Federalist* 17. Madison made much the same argument in number 46.
[3] *The Federalist* 45.
[4] *The Federalist* 17.

it an offense for a farmer to grow wheat—including wheat to be fed to his own livestock or to be ground into flour and made into bread for his own family—in excess of a quota established by a federal government agency; and in 1969 the Court held that a snack bar in a remote recreational facility on a small Arkansas lake, miles from any interstate highway or even major state road and reachable only on country roads, was nevertheless engaged in interstate commerce insofar as it affected this commerce within the meaning of the Civil Rights Act of 1964.[5] There can be little doubt that if, as the advocates of the cause of the states have argued at least since Jefferson's 1791 opinion on the constitutionality of the bank, and as Madison and Hamilton seem to concede in certain passages of *The Federalist,* the Framers of the Constitution intended the powers of the federal government to be "few and defined" and to be "exercised principally on external objects, [such] as war, peace, negotiation, and foreign commerce,"[6] then surely our history demonstrates that the fears of 1788 were not unfounded and that the charges of federal usurpation, leveled by Jefferson and by Madison himself, in 1798, and by others down into the present day, are not without merit. Whether they have this merit depends on the intended meaning of the Constitution as a whole. While in one sense the meaning of the Tenth Amendment, the subject of this paper, is obvious and beyond dispute, in another sense whatever meaning it has depends altogether on the meaning of the Constitution as a whole, and it will be necessary to address this larger question. Those who invoke the Tenth Amendment in order to resist federal power belong to the states-sovereignty school of the Constitution (although, as we shall see, their reliance on the Amendment can only mean their abandonment of the essential element in the states-sovereignty theory).

## II

The enactment of the infamous Alien and Sedition Laws provoked Jefferson and Madison's charges of federal usurpation in their Kentucky and Virginia Resolutions of 1798. The so-called Tariff of

[5] Wickard v. Filburn, 317 U.S. 111 (1942); Daniel v. Paul, 395 U.S. 298 (1969).
[6] *The Federalist* 45.

Abominations of 1828 and the somewhat less "abominable" tariff of 1832 were followed by South Carolina's Ordinance of Nullification; and the 1954 Supreme Court decision in *Brown v. Board of Education,* the school segregation case, was followed by various southern protests, including James Jackson Kilpatrick's *The Sovereign States: Notes of a Citizen of Virginia.*[1] In each case, as well as in others, the exercise of federal power brought forth not only a protest but a statement, or restatement, of the states-sovereignty theory of the Constitution.

This theory rests on a series of related propositions, the first of which being that it was the individual and separate states, not "one people," that declared independence of Great Britain, from which it follows that the states preceded the United States in time. Thus, or so it is alleged, the states, and not "we the people," created the United States, and more specifically, the United States is a compact entered into by the sovereign states with each other. The states and the United States stand in the legal relation of principal and agent, and the Constitution is the agreement stating the terms of the relationship. Whenever the agent, the United States, exceeds the terms of the agreement, it is the right of each of the principals, that is, each sovereign state, so to declare. This declaration may assume the form of an "interposition," a "nullification," or, in the extreme case, an abrogation (with notice) of the agreement itself, otherwise known as secession.

The advocates of states sovereignty, as well as their opponents, have always known that clashes of authority are inevitable—indeed, it would be disingenuous for anyone addressing himself to the question of a federal union to deny the possibility, in fact, the inevitability, of disputes concerning the legitimate extent of federal and state authority; they have always known, therefore, that the decisive question is who is to arbitrate these disputes. The essence of states sovereignty consists in the proposition that it is the right of the states to perform the role of arbiter or judge. Jefferson declared in the first of the Kentucky Resolutions,

> ... that the Government created by this compact was not made the exclusive or final *judge* of the extent of the

[1] James Jackson Kilpatrick, *The Sovereign States: Notes of a Citizen of Virginia* (Chicago: Henry Regnery Company, 1957).

powers delegated to itself; since that would have made its discretion, and not the Constitution, the measure of its powers; but that as in all other cases of compact among parties having no common Judge, each party has an equal right to judge for itself, as well of infractions as of the mode and measure of redress.

Madison, in the Virginia Resolutions, made the same point: "... in case of a deliberate, palpable, and dangerous exercise of other powers not granted by the said compact, the States, who are parties thereto, have the right and are in duty bound to interpose for arresting the progress of the evil. ..." The decisive role of the states is claimed more emphatically in his 1799 Report on the Resolutions: "The states then, being the parties to the constitutional compact, and in their sovereign capacity, it follows of necessity that there can be no tribunal above their authority to decide, in the last resort, whether the compact made by them be violated. ..."[8] The function performed historically by the Supreme Court of the United States belongs by right, according to the doctrine of states sovereignty, to the individual states.

## III

It will be necessary to return briefly to the subject of states sovereignty in the concluding section of this paper, but here it must be pointed out that the meaning of the Tenth Amendment assumes importance, as we said above, only after the essence of the states-sovereignty doctrine has been abandoned. The reason for this is almost obvious: if the states themselves were intended to be the judges of the legitimate extent of their own and of federal power (if, for example, the Constitution contained a provision authorizing the state legislatures to exercise a kind of review of federal legislation), they would not require a tenth amendment to remind them that they intended, when they established the Constitution, to set limits to their agent's (that is, the federal government's) power. Under this condition, there would be no need of a tenth amend-

---

[8] For an example of the application of this theory, see South Carolina's "Ordinance to Nullify certain acts of the Congress of the United States, purporting to be laws laying duties and imposts on the importation of foreign commodities," enacted November 24, 1832, and printed in Commager, *Documents of American History* (New York: F. S. Crofts & Company, 1934), Vol. I, pp. 261–62.

ment. Thus, by taking a stand on the ground of the Amendment, the states-rights advocates have retreated to a second line of defense: they have conceded, whether they realize it or not, the right of the federal government, and in practice the Supreme Court, to arbitrate federal-state relations. The Tenth Amendment would make no sense as an admonition addressed to the states. It can be understood only as an admonition to the Supreme Court that the federal government may not legitimately exercise all the powers of government.

According to Chief Justice Stone in his opinion for the Court in *United States* v. *Darby,* the

> amendment states but a truism that all is retained which has not been surrendered. There is nothing in the history of its adoption to suggest that it was more than declaratory of the relationship between the national and state governments as it had been established by the Constitution before the amendment or that its purpose was other than to allay fears that the new national government might seek to exercise powers not granted, and that the states might not be able to exercise fully their reserved powers.[9]

The evidence supports this view of the Amendment.

If, for example, we consult what are widely (but not universally) considered the most authoritative commentaries on the Constitution, we find Joseph Story declaring as follows:

> This amendment is a mere affirmation of what, upon any just reasoning, is a necessary rule of interpreting the constitution. Being an instrument of limited and enumerated powers, it follows irresistibly, that what is not conferred, is withheld, and belongs to the state authorities, if invested by their constitutions of government respectively in them; and if not so invested, it is retained BY THE PEOPLE, as a part of their residuary sovereignty.[10]

Story's first statement deserves comment: he says the Amendment is a mere affirmation of a necessary rule of *interpreting* the Constitution. It is not a rule of the law of the Constitution, which is to say that no court can base its holding in any case on the

[9] 312 U.S. 100. 124 (1941).
[10] Story, *Commentaries on the Constitution of the United States* (1833), Sec. 1900.

144

# The Meaning of the Tenth Amendment

Amendment because the Amendment does not contain terms that can provide a rule of law. In this respect it differs from the commerce clause, for example, which empowers Congress to regulate not all commerce but only some commerce: "The Congress shall have Power... To regulate Commerce with foreign Nations, and among the several States, and with the Indian Tribes." Unlike the Tenth Amendment, which merely declares that what is not granted is reserved, the commerce clause specifies what commercial powers are granted and, implicitly, what commercial powers are reserved, and thereby provides the terms in which the constitutionality of congressional legislation can be determined. That is to say, a litigant can challenge an Act of Congress that purports to be a regulation of commerce with the argument that the activity being regulated is not commercial in nature, or if commercial, is not commerce with foreign nations or among the several states or with the Indian tribes, but is rather part of that commerce regulation of which is, by the commerce clause itself, reserved to the states.

The Tenth Amendment, on the other hand, contains no terms that the courts can use to settle any legal case or controversy. Litigants have referred to it in the course of resisting the exercise of federal power, but, since every Act of Congress is alleged to rest on some specific power-granting clause, courts have been required to look to those other clauses to determine whether the power being exercised is authorized; that is, to look to other clauses, such as the commerce clause, for the rules by which cases can be decided. Thus, it is not by chance that in the annotated Constitution, 147 pages are devoted to commerce clause cases decided by the Supreme Court, and only eight to cases in which the Tenth Amendment is referred to, and in the latter cases the references occur in the context of interpreting other parts of the Constitution.[11] In Thomas Reed Powell's words, the Tenth Amendment is a "canon of political policy [that] may carry a counsel of caution in deciding whether some proposed measure is really within or without the scope of national authority."[12] It is an accessory to interpretation of the Constitution;

[11] *The Constitution of the United States of America: Analysis and Interpretation* (Washington: Government Printing Office, 1964).
[12] "Child Labor, Congress and the Constitution," 3 *Selected Essays on Constitutional Law* 527–28.

it is not and cannot provide a rule of law of the Constitution.

After alluding to the debate in the First Congress on the Amendment, to which we shall refer below. Story concludes his commentary on this part of the Constitution in these words:

> It is plain . . . that it could not have been the intention of the framers of this amendment to give it effect, as an abridgment of any of the powers granted under the constitution, whether they are express or implied, direct or incidental. Its sole design is to exclude any interpretation, by which other powers should be assumed beyond those, which are granted. All that are granted in the original instrument, whether express or implied, whether direct or incidental, are left in their original state. . . . The attempts, then, which have been made from time to time, to force upon this language an abridging, or restrictive influence, are utterly unfounded in any just rule of interpreting the words, or the sense of the instrument. Stripped of the ingenious disguises in which they are clothed, they are neither more nor less than attempts to foist into the text the word "expressly"; to qualify what is general, and obscure what is clear and defined.[13]

The attempts to which Story refers have succeeded more than once in our constitutional history, and it is largely from them that the Amendment has become a matter of controversy.

In the early case of *Calder* v. *Bull,* the Supreme Court had to decide whether a Connecticut legislative enactment setting aside a decree of a probate court constituted an ex post facto law and was therefore void under Article I, Section 9, of the Constitution. In the course of deciding in favor of the state legislature, Justice Samuel Chase, in a wholly unnecessary dictum (for the decision turned on the meaning of ex post facto), declared that "all the powers delegated by the people of the United States to the federal government are defined, and no *constructive* powers can be exercised by it,"[14] which means that the federal government is limited to the exercise of those powers *expressly* delegated to it by the Constitution. But it

[13] Story, *op. cit.,* Sec. 1901. Story is referring to the fact that the Articles of Confederation contained, in a clause otherwise similar to the Tenth Amendment, the word "expressly." This matter is discussed below.
[14] 3 Dall. 386, 387 (1798).

is emphatically not true that all the powers of the federal government are "defined" in the Constitution—unless the word "defined" is used so loosely as to deprive it of all meaning. Rather, it is emphatically true that the full scope of federal power can be determined only by "construction"—reasonable construction, but construction nevertheless. The reference here is, of course, to the last clause of Article I, Section 8, wherein Congress is given the power to "make all Laws which shall be necessary and proper for carrying into Execution the foregoing Powers, and all other Powers vested by this Constitution in the Government of the United States, or in any Department or Officer thereof."[15] Powers that are "necessary and proper for carrying into Execution" other powers that are expressly granted cannot be said to be "defined," at least not in themselves; if they are defined at all, it is only by reference to something else, and the referring terms, "necessary and proper," are not lacking in ambiguity. What is necessary and proper, furthermore, is a matter requiring "construction."

What Chase did implicitly in *Calder* v. *Bull,* namely, to "foist" the word "expressly" into the text of the Tenth Amendment, was done explicitly by later Supreme Court justices. The 1868 case of *Lane County* v. *Oregon* involved the issuance of $150 million in federal notes, which, according to the Act of Congress, were to be "receivable in payment of all taxes . . . to the United States," with one exception, and were to be regarded as "lawful money and legal tender in payment of all debts, public and private, within the United States," with another exception not relevant to the case. Oregon subsequently passed a law requiring sheriffs to pay over to the county treasurers "the full amount of the state and school taxes, in gold and silver coin"; and the county treasurers to pay over to the state treasurer "the State tax in gold and silver coin." Lane County tendered the amount due to the state in United States notes, and the state sued to recover the full amount in gold and silver coin, as required by state law. The state court awarded judgment to the

[15] It was a part of the politics of states rights to ignore this clause when defining federal power. Mr. Kilpatrick quotes—with approval—the statement of Judge William Cabell in the Virginia court in the Fairfax lands case to the effect that to "the Federal government are confided certain powers, specially enumerated. . . ." Kilpatrick, *op. cit.,* p. 122.

state, and Lane County appealed to the federal Supreme Court on the grounds that its tender of United States notes was warranted by the Act of Congress and that the state law, if construed to require payment only in coin, was repugnant to the Act of Congress. The Supreme Court affirmed the judgment below by denying that Congress in the legal-tender statute had intended to include taxes imposed by state authority, which meant that there was no conflict between the congressional statute and the state law. In his opinion for a unanimous Court, Chief Justice Salmon P. Chase (not the Chase of *Calder* v. *Bull*), found it expedient to make some general and, under the circumstances, unnecessary references to the Constitution. "But in many articles of the Constitution," he wrote, "the necessary existence of the States, and, within their proper sphere, the independent authority of the States, is distinctly recognized. To them nearly the whole charge of interior regulation is committed or left; to them and to the people all powers not *expressly* delegated to the national government are reserved."[16]

Once again the decision did not turn on the meaning of the Tenth Amendment but, in this case, on the meaning of a statute. Yet it is worth noting that the Chief Justice, in giving the Act of Congress the narrowest of interpretations so as to uphold the right of the state to require its taxes to be paid in coin, saw fit to "foist into the text the word 'expressly,' " which, as we shall see, the framers of the Amendment were very careful to keep out of the text.

The third and most famous (or infamous) case in this line of Tenth Amendment decisions is *Hammer* v. *Dagenhart*. The statute attacked in this case was an Act of Congress prohibiting, not the production of goods by child labor, but merely the shipment of such goods into another state (or, more precisely, the offering for such shipment of such goods). The Supreme Court, in an opinion by Justice Day that has been subjected to more devastating criticism than perhaps any opinion ever written by a Supreme Court justice with the possible exception of Taney's opinion for the Court in *Dred Scott* v. *Sandford*, denied that the power to regulate commerce among the states included the power to prohibit commerce—in spite

[16] 7 Wall. 71, 76 (1868). Italics supplied.

148

of the fact that the Court had recently upheld the prohibition of interstate commerce in lottery tickets, to name only one item, which Day distinguished with a wholly specious argument, and in spite of the fact that Jefferson's administration had prohibited *all* foreign commerce, on the basis of the authority given Congress by the same clause that Congress relied on here. Justice Day saw the law to be an attempt on the part of Congress to force the states to abolish child labor (although, strictly speaking, its effect was merely to deny to a manufacturer the benefits of commerce outside his state if he employed children), and declared that the "grant of authority over a purely federal matter was not intended to destroy the local power always existing and carefully reserved to the States in the Tenth Amendment to the Constitution."[17] One page later he wrote as follows:

> In interpreting the Constitution it must never be forgotten that the Nation is made up of States to which are entrusted the powers of local government. And to them and to the people the powers not *expressly* delegated to the National Government are reserved. *Lane County* v. *Oregon,* 7 Wall. 71, 76. The power of the States to regulate their purely internal affairs by such laws as seem wise to the local authority is inherent and has never been surrendered to the general government.[18]

As Holmes pointed out in his powerful dissent (concurred in by three other members of the Court), the matter being regulated here was not an internal affair; the statute became operative only when a local manufacturer sought to "foist" his products onto the out-of-state market. And once again it should be noted that the citing of the Tenth Amendment was accompanied by a distortion of its text, by, that is, the foisting "into the text the word 'expressly.' " Once again it is proper to point out that the decision turned on the interpretation of another clause in the Constitution—here the commerce clause; and it should be plain from Day's language quoted above that the Tenth Amendment does not provide a rule of law

[17] 247 U.S. 251, 274 (1918).
[18] 247 U.S. 251, 275. Italics supplied.

out, instead, a rule of interpretation. And, once again, the application of this rule was accompanied by the distortion of the text of the Amendment. Reference to the Amendment in the context of denying federal power does not require such distortion; that is, it is surely possible in the course of determining the extent of federal power to be guided by the "counsel of caution" that the federal government is one of limited powers, without having to distort the text.[19] Just as surely, the United States is left with fewer powers if the states (and the people) are said to have reserved all powers not *expressly* delegated to it. In fact, the application of this judicially-amended rule of interpretation seems to lead, as it did in *Hammer* v. *Dagenhart,* to a denial of a power that *is* expressly delegated. Mr. Kilpatrick is absolutely correct when he says that the "Supreme Court . . . has no authority to repeal any provision of the Constitution. . . . [And] so long as the Tenth Amendment remains a part of the Constitution, it is elementary that it must be given full meaning. . . ."[20] But neither does the Supreme Court have the authority to amend the Constitution by adding words to it and then giving a full meaning to the amended Amendment—especially when the framers of the Amendment were unusually careful to omit the very word added by the Court in these three cases.

In his famous opinion for the full Court in *McCulloch* v. *Maryland,* Chief Justice Marshall, in the course of determining the scope of Congress's power under the "necessary and proper" clause, stressed the fact that, unlike the similar clause in the Articles of Confederation, the Tenth Amendment does not include the word "expressly." "The men who drew and adopted this amendment," Marshall declared, "had experienced the embarrassments resulting from the insertion of this word in the Articles of Confederation, and

---

[19] See, for instance, *Civil Rights Cases,* 109 U.S. 3 (1883), and *Schechter Poultry Corp.* v. *United States,* 295 U.S. 495 (1935). In another case, one that can be said to come closer than any other to relying on the Tenth Amendment for its rule of decision, *Collector* v. *Day,* 11 Wall. 113 (1871), Justice Nelson correctly quotes the Amendment (p. 124), but on the next page he quotes, with obvious approval, Chase's misquotation in *Lane County* v. *Oregon.* He then goes on to hold that Congress has no power to impose an income tax on the salary of a state judge—an absurd decision that was overruled in *Graves* v. *O'Keefe,* 306 U.S. 466 (1939).

[20] Kilpatrick, *op. cit.,* p. 47.

probably omitted it to avoid those embarrassments."[21] But the states-rights advocates are never willing to accept Marshall's credentials as constitutional expositor. "To be sure," Mr. Kilpatrick writes of his fellow Virginian's opinion, "John Marshall, not long after the Union was formed, was to seize upon the fact that the restriction went only to the 'powers not delegated,' and not to the 'powers not *expressly* delegated,' as if this made some large difference."[22] But it made a difference to James Madison (whose credentials *are* accepted by Mr. Kilpatrick) and to a majority of the House of Representatives who, in 1789, in the First Congress, formally proposed the Tenth Amendment. Responding to the motion of South Carolina's Tucker to amend the proposed amendment by adding the word "expressly," Madison said he objected to the addition "because it was impossible to confine a Government to the exercise of express powers; [and because] there must necessarily be admitted powers by implication, unless the constitution descended to recount every minutia." The debate that ensued was very short, not one rising to support Tucker, and the motion was lost without a taking of the yeas and nays.[23] On the basis of this evidence one would be entitled to argue that Madison and his fellow members of the First Congress made a serious mistake, but it is not legitimate to argue that they made it unwittingly and without being aware of the significant difference between the Amendment as it appears in the Constitution and the Amendment as it appears in Tucker's version, in at least three Supreme Court decisions, and in the constitution propounded by Mr. Kilpatrick and his fellow advocates of states sovereignty.

By this time it should be obvious that there can be no legitimate dispute concerning the meaning of the Tenth Amendment: it is merely declaratory of the division of powers between nation and states made in the original, unamended Constitution. This much

[21] 4 Wheat. 316, 406–7 (1819). Article II of the Articles of Confederation reads as follows: "Each state retains its sovereignty, freedom and independence, and every Power, Jurisdiction and right, which is not by this Confederation expressly delegated to the United States, in Congress assembled."

[22] Kilpatrick, *op. cit.*, p. 47.

[23] *Annals of Congress*, Vol. I, p. 790.

was conceded by counsel for the state of Maryland in its great dispute with the Bank of the United States in *McCulloch* v. *Maryland:* "We admit, that the Tenth Amendment to the Constitution is merely declaratory; that it was adopted *ex abundanti cautela* [out of an abundance of caution]; and that with it nothing more is reserved than would have been reserved without it."[24] The only legitimate dispute, and the focus of that case, is the division of powers made in the unamended Constitution, and specifically, the effect of the "necessary and proper" clause on that division. What is not delegated to the United States is, without question—for the Tenth Amendment so declares—reserved to the states or to the people; but among the powers delegated is the power to make all laws that are "necessary and proper for carrying into Execution" all the other powers expressly granted. As to the meaning of the Tenth Amendment, then, there can be no doubt; but what are necessary and proper laws is a question on which honest and intelligent men can differ and have differed throughout our constitutional history. And nowhere in this history has this question been so fully argued and so uncompromisingly answered as in the case of *McCulloch* v. *Maryland*. This question, fraught with such divergent tendencies, makes the decision in this case one of the most important decisions, if not *the* most important decision, ever handed down by the Court.

*McCulloch* v. *Maryland* involved the constitutionality of a Maryland tax levied on all notes issued by banks other than those chartered by the state, unless such banks paid annually the sum of $15,000 to the state. McCulloch was the cashier of the Baltimore branch of the Bank of the United States who refused to pay the tax, and the state sued to recover the statutory penalties. Judgment was rendered against him in the state court and, after affirmance by the Maryland Court of Appeals, he sued out a writ of error to the Supreme Court of the United States. The first question, and the only one directly relevant to this discussion, was whether Congress has the power to incorporate a bank. The question was not new in 1819, for it had been asked of Hamilton, Jefferson, and Randolph by President Washington in 1791 after Congress had passed a bill establishing the first Bank of the United States; and the significance

[24] 4 Wheat. 316, 363 (1819).

of the Court's decision in 1819 is best grasped by reading the answers of Hamilton and Jefferson to Washington's question, because in those answers is to be found the essence of the national-state dispute: disagreement on the kind of country intended by the Framers of the Constitution. In Hamilton's view, the principles by which Jefferson construed the various provisions of the Constitution "would be fatal to the just and indispensable authority of the United States."[25] And so they would—to his United States. In Jefferson's view, a principle of constitutional construction that would permit Congress to incorporate a bank "would reduce the whole instrument to a single phrase, that of instituting a Congress with power to do whatever would be for the good of the United States,"[26] and that Congress should have such powers implied a nation that, according to his principles, was incompatible with republican government.

This disagreement on the constitutionality of the Bank is usually described in terms of liberal or loose as opposed to strict construction of the Constitution, and it was this, certainly. Hamilton, starting from the proposition that the powers of the national government are sovereign as to those objects "intrusted to its management," and that these sovereign powers include the means requisite to the ends of the powers, unless specifically denied in the Constitution, or immoral, or "contrary to the *essential ends* of political society," concludes that the power "to erect a corporation" is a sovereign power. This does not mean that Congress may erect a corporation "for superintending the police of the city of Philadelphia," because Congress is "not authorized to *regulate* the *police* of that city." But Congress, because it is expressly authorized to "lay and collect taxes," may certainly establish a bank to facilitate the exercise of this power. A bank is not "absolutely or indispensably" necessary to collect taxes, but the true construction of the word "necessary" in the "necessary and proper" clause, in the grammatical as well as the popular sense of the word, is "*needful, requisite, incidental, useful,* or *conducive to.*" The degree to which "a measure is necessary can never be a

---

[25] "Opinion as to the Constitutionality of the Bank of the United States," in *Works of Alexander Hamilton,* Lodge ed. (1885), Vol. III, p. 180.
[26] "Opinion on the Constitutionality of a National Bank," in *The Writings of Thomas Jefferson,* Ford ed., Vol. V, p. 286.

*test* of the legal right to adopt it; that must be a matter of opinion, and can only be a *test* of expediency."

To Jefferson, the power to incorporate a bank was not among the enumerated powers, and the carrying "into execution" of the "enumerated powers" does not require a bank. A bank may be convenient in that its bills "would have a currency all over the States," but by the same argument it would be "still more convenient" to have a bank, "whose bills should have a currency all over the world," and it certainly "does not follow from this superior conveniency, that there exists anywhere a power to establish such a bank...." The Constitution restricts Congress "to the *necessary* means, that is to say, to those means without which the grant of power would be nugatory."[27]

Thus, their dispute narrows down to, and the effect of the Tenth Amendment depends on, the meaning of the word *necessary*, whether it should be construed loosely or strictly. This cannot be answered by an application of the principles of grammar or even of philology; on the contrary, the answer must be obtained by the rules applicable to the interpretation of legal documents, which Jefferson then stated in a wholly unobjectionable form: "It is," he said, "an established rule of construction, where a phrase will bear either of two meanings, to give it that which will allow some meaning to the other parts of the instrument, and not that which would render all the others useless." But what is the meaning of the Constitution? That is, what is the purpose of the Constitution? The fundamental dispute underlying the grammatical disagreement concerns the purpose of the Constitution or, in short, the kind of country the United States was intended to be. It was because John Marshall and his associates on the Supreme Court agreed with Hamilton's view of the nature of the United States that they adopted his interpretation of the "necessary and proper" clause in their decision on the Bank in *McCulloch* v. *Maryland*, and held the incorporating of a bank to be among the powers of Congress and the Maryland tax to be illegal. It was because they shared his view of the nature, or character, of the United States that they never added the word "expressly" to the Tenth Amendment; and, because so much of

[27] Cf. Madison's statement in the debate on the Tenth Amendment, p. 151 above.

# The Meaning of the Tenth Amendment

Marshall's opinion for the Court is taken bodily from Hamilton's opinion on the constitutionality of the Bank, it is inconceivable that they were not cognizant of the alternatives between which they had to choose, for these alternatives are readily seen by comparing Hamilton's opinion with Jefferson's.

Hamilton's United States enacts laws whose objects are "to give encouragement to the enterprise of our own merchants, and to advance our navigation and manufactures." Commerce is to be the way of the nation and "money is the very hinge on which commerce turns." It is banks that provide the money, not only in the form of loans, but also in the form of notes circulating as a credit upon the coin and other property deposited with them. Banks facilitate commerce, they provide the credit needed for commerce; indeed, Congress' power to regulate commerce authorizes it to erect a corporation whose purpose is, by collecting the capital of a number of individuals, to permit the development of a "new and unexplored branch of trade . . . with some foreign country." This United States is necessarily to be heavily involved in foreign affairs, which makes war a likely possibility, and banks are a convenient source of the loans needed to fight wars. (And when the United States conquers in these wars, it will not be doubted that it possesses "sovereign jurisdiction over the conquered territory," a jurisdiction "competent to any species of legislation.") This is an aggressive country, busily and extensively engaged in many affairs, of growing authority in the world of business and the world of nations. It requires an active government with sufficient powers to provide direction and to promote its interests. "The means by which *national* exigencies are to be provided for, *national* inconveniences obviated, *national* prosperity promoted, are of such infinite variety, extent, and complexity, that there must of necessity be a great latitude of discretion in the selection and application of those means."[28] The powers attached, of necessity in Hamilton's view, to the office of the presidency of such a country are broad enough to promote the national interest, broad enough, in fact, to permit scope for statesmanship as this was traditionally understood. "If the *end* be clearly comprehended within any of the specified powers, and if the measure have an obvious relation

[28] Italics supplied.

to that *end,* and is not forbidden by any particular provision of the Constitution, it may safely be deemed to come within the compass of the national authority." Marshall's version of this in his opinion upholding the constitutionality of the Second Bank, reads as follows: "Let the end be legitimate, let it be within the scope of the constitution, and all means which are appropriate, which are plainly adapted to that end, which are not prohibited, but consist with the letter and spirit of the constitution, are constitutional."[29]

Counsel for the state of Maryland knew what was at stake in the case, what hinged on its outcome. "To derive such a tremendous authority from implication," he pleaded, "would be . . . to change the whole scheme and theory of the government."[30] But by 1819, the nation had probably been irreversibly set in the Hamiltonian direction, despite the rhetoric of the Jacksonians, and the question before the Court was more likely whether an attempt should be made to turn it around. There is no question but that Jefferson's United States lay in the opposite direction. This is to be seen in his insistence that the powers of the national government be restricted to those enumerated plus those absolutely and indispensably needed to carry into execution those that were enumerated; in his theory of the presidency with authority only to execute the laws; and mostly in his insistence, stemming from Rousseau, that republican government was possible only in a simple society marked by an equality of conditions. Such a society would be based on agriculture. Thus, it was altogether consistent for him to resist the Bank and the theory of the Constitution that authorized its incorporation, on the ground that the Bank bill toppled the "pillars of our whole system of jurisprudence," the "most ancient and fundamental laws of the several States; such as those against Mortmain, the laws of Alienage, the rules of descent, the acts of distribution, the laws of escheat and forfeiture, the laws of monopoly."

The Bank bill, in short, and in Jefferson's opinion, broke down the basic laws of an agricultural society, one of them at least deriving from feudal times, and, with the exception of the laws of distribution and the laws preventing monopoly, all of them dealing with real property. Banks promoted other kinds of property and another

[29] 4 Wheat. 316, 421 (1819).
[30] *Ibid.,* p. 365.

# The Meaning of the Tenth Amendment

kind of United States. A bill to incorporate a national bank was contrary to the spirit of the Constitution, because it fostered a way of life contrary to the one intended by the Framers as he understood it. More particularly, the Bank bill was in conflict with the "most ancient and fundamental laws of the several States," and was therefore unconstitutional. He advised President Washington accordingly.

Washington, however, signed the bill into law and the Marshall court upheld the constitutionality of the Second Bank, because, in part, Marshall and his colleagues agreed with the theory of constitutional construction advanced by Madison in Congress during the debate on the Bank bill in 1791: "Interference with the power of the States was no constitutional criterion of the power of Congress." If the power was not given, Madison continued, "Congress could not exercise it; if given, they might exercise it, although it should interfere with the laws, or even the Constitution of the States."[31] And Marshall and his colleagues agreed with this theory of constitutional construction because they agreed with Hamilton's view of the United States:

> Throughout this vast republic, from the St. Croix to the Gulph of Mexico, from the Atlantic to the Pacific, revenue is to be collected and expended, armies are to be marched and supported. The exigencies of the nation may require, that the treasure raised in the north should be transported to the south, that raised in the east conveyed to the west, or that this order should be reversed. Is that construction of the constitution to be preferred which would render these operations difficult, hazardous, and expensive? Can we adopt that construction (unless the words imperiously

[31] *Writings,* Hunt, ed., Vol. VI, p. 28. But Madison opposed the Bank bill because, he said, the power to incorporate it was not given. Whether this was consistent with his argument against the attempt to add the word "expressly" to the Tenth Amendment, we need not consider, for Madison was anything but consistent. True, his opposition to a bank of the United States did not change, but in a letter to Spencer Roane of September 2, 1819, he said, in the course of denouncing the Court's decision in *McCulloch* v. *Maryland,* that the "very existence of [the states] is a control on the pleas for a constructive amplification of the powers of the General Government" —that is, the mere existence of the states is a limitation on the powers of the national government. This is a direct contradiction of his statement during the 1791 debate on the Bank bill.

require it) which would impute to the framers of that instrument, when granting these powers for the public good, the intention of impeding their exercise by withholding a choice of means?[32]

## IV

We have argued in this paper that the meaning of the Tenth Amendment is beyond legitimate dispute, that it is merely declaratory of the distribution of powers made in the original Constitution, that the attempts to rely on it for a rule of constitutional law rather than of construction require a distortion of the text, and that the decisive argument concerns the meaning of the "necessary and proper" clause. We have argued further that the meaning of this clause hinges on the intent of the Framers. Did they intend to establish a simple society based on an equality of conditions (and not a society whose government has as its "first object . . . the protection of different and unequal faculties of acquiring property"),[33] a simple society made possible and maintained by a life devoted to agriculture and a passive government, or, on the contrary, a busy commercial society, based on trade and manufacturing, and requiring an active, aggressive, powerful government? Assuming that the Constitution itself would lend itself to either of these diverse and incompatible ways of life, and assuming that the issue had not yet been decided in 1791 at the time of the debate on the constitutionality of the Bank, indeed, that it had still to be decided with finality in 1819 at the time of *McCulloch* v. *Maryland,* can there be any doubt that today the decision has long since been made? Is it not inconceivable today, and has it not been so for a long time, that the national interest of the United States can be promoted (and who does not want to promote it?) by a government restricted to the exercise of those powers "absolutely and indispensably" necessary?

This is an argument from necessity and not an argument based on the intrinsic merits of such a government. It is an argument that does not palliate the discontent of the advocates of states rights who continue to insist not only that it might have been otherwise,

[32] *McCulloch* v. *Maryland,* 4 Wheat. 316, 408 (1819).
[33] *The Federalist* 10.

but that it was intended to be otherwise: Mr. Kilpatrick, in 1957, long after the decisive battle had been fought, entitled his book *The Sovereign States: Notes of a Citizen of Virginia*. In it he insists not only that the Tenth Amendment was intended to place stringent limitations on the national government, not only that the word *necessary* was intended to mean absolutely necessary, but that the states were intended to arbitrate disputes between national and state governments: he contends for the states-sovereignty doctrine in its entirety by arguing that *Martin* v. *Hunter's Lessee* was decided incorrectly. This assertion deserves a brief response.

One of the lengthy debates in the First Congress came on the bill to establish a federal judiciary, although the only extended discussion was devoted to the part that was to become Section 3 of the Judiciary Act of 1789, the section providing for the establishment of the federal district courts. There were vigorous arguments against such establishment and in favor of reliance on the existing state court systems, yet the motion in the House to strike the provision from the bill was defeated 11-31.[34] On the all-important Section 25, which authorizes the Supreme Court to review and reverse the judgments of the state courts,[35] no debate took place; or if it took place, it was not recorded. But is not the deed, even without the words, significant, perhaps even conclusive, since so many members of Congress had been delegates to the Constitutional Convention, and can be presumed to have known what they were doing? And what they did was to establish the Supreme Court as arbiter of the conflicts between state and national laws, between state laws and the federal Constitution and treaties made under the authority of the United States. The states-sovereignty doctrine cannot exist with this law of the First Congress, so that when Virginia found itself involved

[34] *Annals of Congress,* Vol. I, p. 866.
[35] "Sec. 25: *And be it further enacted,* That a final judgment or decree in any suit, in the highest court of law or equity of a State in which a decision in the suit could be had, where is drawn in question the validity of a treaty or statute of, or an authority exercised under the United States, and the decision is against their validity; or where is drawn in question the validity of a statute of, or an authority exercised under any State, on the ground of their being repugnant to the constitution, treaties or laws of the United States, and the decision is in favour of such their validity ... may be re-examined and reversed or affirmed in the Supreme Court of the United States upon a writ of error...."

in the struggle over the ownership of the Fairfax lands, and its highest court refused to obey the mandate of the Supreme Court of the United States, it did so by denying the constitutionality of this section of the Judiciary Act. This judgment was reversed by a unanimous Supreme Court in the famous case of *Martin* v. *Hunter's Lessee* in 1816, in an opinion written by Madison's appointee to the Court, Joseph Story.[36]

This settled the matter, so far as the law of the Constitution is concerned; it did not settle the matter so far as Mr. Kilpatrick is concerned. He is one of "many Americans . . . who pray earnestly that one day the fight may be resumed."[37] But of him and those who would fight this battle with him, we would ask whether any other decision, in 1816 or at any other time, past or future, would be compatible with the second clause of Article VI—not of the Articles of Confederation but of the Constitution of the United States—which provides that "this Constitution, and the Laws of the United States which shall be made in Pursuance thereof; and all Treaties made, or which shall be made, under the Authority of the United States, shall be the supreme law of the Land; and the Judges in every State shall be bound thereby, any Thing in the Constitution or Laws of any State to the Contrary notwithstanding."

And we would also direct their attention to one of the major ironies of American history: Jefferson, by purchasing Louisiana, did more than anyone to bring about a country extending from "sea to shining sea" and unable to avoid a place among the major powers of the world, thereby rendering impossible his dream of a simple, Rousseauian republic whose life was to be based on the land and whose government was to be restricted to a few enumerated powers. The purchase made a shambles of his constitutional theories, and he knew it; he said the purchase was unconstitutional, but he made it and had to suffer in silence the indignity of listening to his party friends defending his action as an exercise of an authority derived from the "necessary and proper" clause.[38] "Even in 1804,"

---

[36] 1 Wheat. 304 (1816).
[37] Kilpatrick, *op. cit.*, p. 125.
[38] Henry Adams, *History of the United States of America* (New York, 1890), Vol. II, p. 103.

wrote Henry Adams, "the political consequ
already too striking to be overlooked."

> Within three years of his inauguration Jeffe
> foreign colony without its consent and agains
> nexed it to the United States by an act which h
> blank paper of the Constitution; and then he
> found his predecessors too monarchical, and the
> tion too liberal in powers,—made himself monarc
> new territory, and wielded over it, against its prote
> powers of its old kings."[39]

And when Gallatin, his Secretary of the Treasury, took
establish a branch bank of the United States at New Orle
protested that "this institution is one of the most deadly he
existing against the principles and form of our Constitution'
but he acquiesced in its establishment. Henry Adam's comment
the entire episode is singularly appropriate today, and should h
weighed by all those who, like Mr. Kilpatrick, are drawn to the old
cause of their intellectual mentor:

> Such an experience was final; no century of slow and half-
> understood experience could be needed to prove that the
> hopes of humanity lay thenceforward, not in attempting to
> restrain the government from doing whatever the majority
> should think necessary, but in raising the people them-
> selves till they should think nothing necessary but what
> was good.[41]

[39] *Ibid.*, p. 130.
[40] *Ibid.*, p. 131.
[41] *Ibid.*, p. 130.